SHIPLEY GLEN

THE HISTORY AND DEVELOPMENT
OF A VICTORIAN PLAYGROUND

ALAN CATTELL

First published 2018

Published by
Chris Thorpe Graphic Design Ltd
Office 9 - Unit 18,
Calderdale Business Park,
Club Lane, Ovenden,
Halifax HX2 8DS
www.ct-graphicdesign.co.uk   www.bingleyhistoryseries.co.uk
© Alan Cattell, 2018

. . . .

ISBN: 978-0-9956437-2-7

4

CONTENTS

FOREWORD

Shipley Glen has been a popular destination for the people of Bradford for more than 150 years.

Previous Publications

The earliest published account can be found in William Cudworth's *Round about Bradford* published in 1868. This describes the Glen as *'a famous resort in the spring and summer months, and it is as much an 'institution' of Bradford life as Greenwich is of metropolitan'*.

Little more was written until Stanley Varo published *A Shipley Glen Ramble* in 1984. At that time, many people had memories of school and Sunday school trips to the Glen, and their parents had more vivid memories of the various attractions which had some years earlier been demolished. The excellent map in this book has been the basis of many local history walks, including our own.

This volume and the publication *100 Years at Shipley Glen - The Story of the Glen Tramway* (Mick Leak - 2003 plus later additions) have until now been the 'go to' books for anyone wishing to find out about the history of Shipley Glen.

This Book

In this new publication Alan Cattell (who has previously published books and articles which cover various aspects of the history of the Glen) has built on the topics covered in these previous works and added new material. Through extensive research - (particularly using contemporary newspaper articles) he charts the social and commercial changes which influenced the popularity of this area.

In doing so he has woven together the various strands of the Glen's history from its early days to the present, covering themes ranging from ownership of the Glen, farms and farmhouse teas, to the Saltaire Exhibition and the rise and demise of Fairs and permanent rides on the Glen plateau.

The largest strand covers the Victorian and Edwardian heydays of entertainment on the Glen, which at that time was well enough known to be the subject of a music hall song.

The book also includes a detailed Chronological Timeline of events and reference to the hopes and aspirations of the current businesses/ volunteer organisations which still operate on the Glen plateau.

In our opinion the book is very well written and researched and will become the go to book for anyone interested in the history of Shipley Glen.

Mike Lawson - Convener Baildon Local History Society and Tish Lawson - Trustee - The Glen Tramway Preservation Company Ltd

FOREWORD

The second Foreword to this book is written by Sallie Eastell who was born on Shipley Glen and who captures what living and growing up on the Glen meant to her as a child. Also see page 30 where Sallie's Grandmother recounts her own childhood when she was born and lived at Old Glen House from 1887:

My name is Sallie Eastell and I was born at 4 Prod Lane or as it was known then, Shipley Glen Nurseries, owned by my family, in 1964. **What a magical place to be born and bred**.

My earliest childhood memories are of living in a house next to the Shipley Glen Pleasure Grounds and Fairground which were owned by the Teale family. In later years I worked there in the snack bar and also in the cafe, making traditional cheese, egg and ham sandwiches.

Downhill, at the bottom of the road was the Glen Tramway. At that time this was our mode of transport to the Coach Road and Saltaire as there were no bus services to Shipley Glen. On Prod Lane, there were also the Japanese Gardens with Swingboats and a boating lake.

At the top of Prod Lane was the Old Glen House which was a lovely cafe where we as children knocked on the door at all times of the day to buy sweets. Mrs Raistrick, the then owner was very patient and so were the peacocks that she bred. They would roam round, and at night you could hear them screeching, warning everybody if there was anybody around that shouldn't have been. After Mrs Raistrick retired, Mr Duggan bought Old Glen House and converted it into a pub. Initially this caused a bit of controversy because the establishment had never sold alcohol and had once been a Temperance house. The conversion was successful and he also turned the old peacock house into a cafe which at that time was run by his wife Bonita.

Weekends and Bank Holidays were always very busy on the Glen. At the Nurseries we had a small ice cream hut which was rented by an Italian lady called Anna and her lovely family. Sometimes an ice cream van would come down the road, trespassing on Anna's pitch. She would rant on in Italian which although I couldn't understand what she was saying, I could pick up that they weren't pleasant words!

At the Nurseries we obviously sold plants, but I also remember an orange juice machine making drinks which we sold by the cup. We also sold fresh tomatoes which my Dad had grown. A regular best seller were Wright's Brandy Snaps which were supplied to us in red metal barrels. They sold really well and I'm glad to say that they are still trading as a company.

We seemed to have such long hot summers then, sometimes accompanied by thunderstorms and heavy rain. I remember one weekend when the heavens opened unexpectedly on visitors who hadn't brought coats or umbrellas. In those days, to protect the boot of our car from dirt from the plants, we lined it with sheets of thin green polythene from a roll. On this particularly rainy, wet weekend we started out by giving a few visitors sheets to cover themselves. However, they ended up becoming a fashion statement, when to try and keep themselves dry, everybody wanted a green polythene sheet to wear.

Nowadays, I'm glad to say, the Glen Tramway still runs. Sadly however, the Japanese Gardens, Shipley Glen Nurseries, Dodgem Cars and Shipley Glen Pleasure Grounds and Fairground have all closed, some of the sites being developed for housing.

What remains is a quieter, beautiful space where you can still breathe the fresh air and enjoy the surroundings. Many people and their families regularly visit the Glen. I still live in the area and feel privileged to do so having also felt the **enchantment** of **growing up there**.

I would like to thank Alan Cattell for relighting my memories of the Glen and keeping them alive by firstly, writing this book and also by asking me to write a Foreword. I hope that in reading the book you too will feel some of the **magic of the Glen** and its **history**.

Sallie Eastell

PREFACE AND INTRODUCTION

Different Names

Shipley Glen - has been known by different names and attributed to different townships over different periods. This and the reasons for doing so will be outlined in the first chapter of this text and from then on I will call it the **Glen**.

Different Activities

As society and tastes have changed, the Glen has also been known at different times and timescales as the venue for a variety of activities which include:

- Church and Sunday School Picnics
- Band of Hope Temperance outings
- Temperance Hotels
- Permanent Tearooms and Gardens
- Political Rallies
- Walks over the moors to Ilkley
- Farm Teas
- Bank Holiday Fairs
- Amusements, Rides and Entertainment

Chronological Timeline

These will be covered in the main body of this book in the order in which they happened and also in the **Chronological Timeline** on pages 122 - 138. The Timeline is useful in identifying a number of historical themes which occurred as a result of notable changes in politics and society.

Themes

These themes inform the structure of the book chapters. They are also intended to help the reader understand the context of how political/social influences at both national and local level shaped the development of the Glen. This context will be outlined at the beginning of each chapter. These themes are:

1840 - 1869	**Early Development of Shipley Glen**
1870 - 1880	**Common Land, Bank Holidays, Moorland Rambles and Fairs**
1881 - 1886	**Temperance Hotels - Changes on the Glen**
1887	**Saltaire Exhibition as the Model for Developing Shipley Glen Rides**
1888 -1898	**The Rides**
1900	**New Century - New Ownership**
1901 - 1905	**Vulcan House and The Japanese Gardens**
1904 - 1906	**The Farms**
1906 - 1921	**The Fairs**
1930s - 2018	**Looking Back to Look Forward** **Looking Forward - The Glen Tramway, Old Glen House, Old Glen Tea Rooms, Bracken Hall House B and B and Bracken Hall Countryside Centre** **Looking Back on Looking Back - A Retrospective Summary**

Development of the Glen

As such the book is intended to tell the story of the development of the Glen from a place **where working people and their families** (originally through church affiliations), could **enjoy fresh air and exercise**, to a much visited and loved place for **amusement and adventure** for thousands of **workers and holidaymakers**.

The **main focus** of the book will be on the range of **refreshment venues, entertainments and rides** which were built on the **Glen plateau** in the **Victorian and Edwardian** periods, and up to 1921. These were intended to cater for a population enjoying the newly found freedom to explore, created by the provision of new rail networks and transport systems.

Previous Publications

The book will also build on the work of Varo (1984) in *Shipley Glen Ramble* and Leak (2003) in *100 Years at Shipley Glen - The Story of the Glen Tramway*. It will also cover some of the information presented in my first book - Cattell (2011) *Bingley and Surrounds - Forgotten Moments from History*, but will also present a substantial amount of newly researched material.

Acknowledgments

In addition to the invaluable support received from my family, a number of people have been significant in the research leading to the publication of this book.

Jane Fielder the Bingley artist and owner of the Bingley Gallery on Park Road is well known for her "Janescape" paintings locally. This book is our third collaboration, two of Jane's existing paintings having being used as my previous book covers. For this book, she visited the site of the Glen Tramway and rode on it on a number of occasions. The front cover represents her unique style in capturing the Tramway and bluebell woods in April 2018.

Tish and Mike Lawson, both Baildon local historians, have played a major role in meeting me on a number of occasions to share their research and to identify key periods and events in the development of Shipley Glen. My thanks to them also for contributing a Foreword to this book.

Sallie Eastell has also contributed a Foreword which celebrates the joys of her childhood living on the Glen, which was a magical experience for her as she grew up. Her family like many others have a long association with the Glen, her Grandfather having originally set up

Eastells Nursery on Prod Lane and having lived there from the 1920s.

Sally, Stuart and Elaine Illingworth of Bracken Hall Farm and Bracken Hall House have also contributed their knowledge and family memories of living and working on the Glen. Thanks to them and the Friends of Bracken Hall Countryside Centre including the Bracken Hall Countryside Centre Manager Richard White for their help.

Mick Leak who ran the Shipley Glen Tramway with his wife Maureen for nearly nine years has been an invaluable source of information, as has Bill Slessor. Thanks to them for proof checking the final draft of this book and advising on corrections/additions. Thanks also to Richard Freeman and the Trustees of Glen Tramway Preservation Society for allowing Chris Thorpe and I, guided access and permission to take photographs of the Tramway.

My thanks also go to Eric Nicholls who has volunteered for a second time to proof-read one of my books.

Thanks to Bingley and District Local History Society and their Stanley Varo collection, Bradford Libraries, Dorothy Burrows, Joanne Crowther, Graham Hall Archives, Peter Grubisic, Mike Lawson, Shipley College-Saltaire Archives, the Telegraph and Argus, Chris Thorpe and Mick Walmsley, for permission to use some of their images.

Thank you also to the many people who lived or worked on the Glen and contributed to its success over many years. This text cannot be exhaustive in naming everyone who did so, but recognises the efforts of those involved in providing a much visited and loved entertainment environment for over 150+ years.

Finally thanks to my publisher Chris Thorpe for his continued support, knowledge, advice and friendship in completing and publishing our fourth book together.

Alan Cattell - August 2018

1 - VICTORIAN ERA
EARLY DEVELOPMENT OF SHIPLEY GLEN 1840 - 1869

What's in a Name?

The area including the Glen has at different times been known by different names and attributed to different townships. These include:

Brackenhall Green (up to around 1852) in Baildon

Eldwick Glen (up to around 1862) near Eldwick

Shipley Glen (first referred to in the Bradford Observer as such in 1863)

Cudworth (1875) in Round about Bradford went as far as to say:

"We come to Shipley Glen as it is wrongfully called, no part of the Glen being within a mile of any part of the township of Shipley... The proper name is Bracken Hall Green and it is in the township of Baildon in the parish of Otley."

Varo (1984) in *Shipley Glen Ramble* observes that on the Ordinance Survey map of 1852, Shipley Glen was not noted. The first specific name given to this area of ground was Brackenhall Green.

Leak (2003) in *100 years at Shipley Glen - The Story of the Glen Tramway* concurs when he states:

"The name Shipley Glen does not exist on the map. The name was coined by the minister of the Bethel Chapel in Shipley. The area is actually composed of Brackenhall Crag and Green, Trench Wood and Walker Wood."

The Leeds Mercury of 5th March, 1881 confirms all the above when it notes:

"The place called Shipley Glen is in the township of Baildon and not at any point connected to the township of Shipley. About forty years ago the place now called Shipley Glen had not the name Glen attached to it. It was then

*called **Brackenhall Green** and was not used as a place of public resort, nor was there any provision for the accommodation of visitors.*

After the Reverend Peter Scott, Baptist Minister of Shipley became acquainted with it and drew the publics' attention to its natural surroundings, it began to be called Shipley Glen, that being the only connection between Shipley and Glen."

What is Shipley Glen Comprised of?

Shipley Glen is an area of outstanding beauty **comprising** the grassy plateau of **Bracken Hall Green**, the spectacular millstone grit **Bracken Hall Crags** and **steeply sloping woodland** on both sides of **Lode Pit (or Loadstone) Beck.**

Change - A Local Context

Several key historic events shaped the early development of the Glen

- The construction of the **railway line to Shipley in 1846**
- The first rail connection into **Bradford in 1846**
- The opening of **Salts Mill in 1853** and the phased building of Saltaire Village commencing 1854
- The opening of **Leeds Station in 1854**
- The opening of **Saltaire Railway Station in 1856**
- The opening of **Ilkley Station in 1865**

Saltaire Station

Courtesy of Shipley College, Saltaire Archives.

Prior to these dates access to this beautiful tract of countryside had essentially only been open to those living in the immediate local area. However from 1846 newspaper records show increasing numbers of people from throughout West Yorkshire were using the embryonic railway system and beginning to walk from Shipley Station and picnic in the area around the Glen. As such the Glen according to newspaper reports was gaining a reputation as:

> **"A favourite retreat of pleasure seekers visited by thousands of persons"**
>
> **"A beautiful place and great source of pleasure and healthy enjoyment"**
>
> **"A place which cannot fail to please and gratify all lovers of nature"**

Conjecture suggests that because of the initial railway access via Shipley, visitors would tell friends that they had "been to Shipley to visit the Glen"...hence **Shipley Glen!**

The Saltaire connection ensured that workers from Salts Mill used the Glen in their few free hours as it was on their doorstep and that at a slightly later stage, the newly opened Saltaire station provided options for increasingly larger numbers of visitors.

However!

In 1854 there were a number of anonymous letters to the Editors of the Leeds Mercury and Bradford Observer newspapers regarding the pro's and con's of conservation versus cultivation of Eldwick Glen and its future development. It was proposed by some that the area be developed as a **"People's Park."**

A Workers Perspective - Public Health

In **1844** a **Royal Commission** had looked into **Sanitary Conditions of Large Towns and Populous Districts.** James Smith reporting to the Commission in 1844 concluded *"...of Bradford I am obliged to pronounce it the most filthy town I visited."*

In **1845** the **Woolcombers Report on Sanitary Conditions in Bradford** was published highlighting the horrifying conditions in which people lived and worked and the low life expectancy of those living there.

Nine years later a letter signed **"An Operative"** sent to the Bradford Observer in April 1854, further captured the continuing problem and contained a plea...which appears to flow from an erudite and well educated pen:

*"I am a **poor man**. I live in a back street where ground is measured out by inches. Dark, ill looking dwellings, the **hotbeds of disease** are my only prospect. What wonder being so cooped up that **I pine for pure air**, for the wide spreading moor and **deep solitary glen**...*

*...I heartily concur in the design to secure Eldwick Glen for the **public benefit**. May the Glen be preserved and the poor man be permitted to **ramble** undisturbed amongst its **many beauties**..."*

In the event the concept of a formal **"People's Park"** did not become a reality but the next phase of the development of the Glen **was** influenced by the political and social needs of workers and their families.

Political and Social Change - A National Context

Besides local influences and changes, several things shaped the early development of the Glen namely:

Mass Meetings

Radical movements for political and social reform for the working man, including action by the Chartists in the period 1838 to 1858, found favour in towns like Bradford and Leeds.

Navickas. K. (2016) in *The Protest and Politics of Space and Place 1789-1849* points out that Radicals during this period were excluded from meeting in civic buildings, pubs or increasingly in town centres. As a result they held **large meetings** in **fields** and on **moors** which were outside the jurisdiction of most urban authorities.

Dingle. A. E. (1980) *The Campaign of Prohibition in Victorian Britain* identifies that **large public meetings** were a central feature of most reforming campaigns in Victorian England. They were a very **visible way of attracting support** and demonstrating to Government the real extent of such support.

Roberts. M. (2008 pp93) *Political Movements in Urban England* observes:
"The attempts by the State to prohibit demonstrations in public places united the various radicals who used these spaces into a broader campaign for the broader issue of rights of assembly and demonstration."

Between 1864 and 1870 **Shipley Glen became a regularly used venue** for Radical Reformers Political Picnics and Working Men's Reform Rallies. Many political and suffrage causes including the Suffragettes in 1908 and 1912 would continue to use the space for mass rallies. In 1908 it was estimated that 100,000 people had attended a Rally at which Emeline Pankhurst was speaking. This was the largest such meeting ever to be held on the Glen.

Sunday School, Temperance and Band of Hope Trips

In Victorian Britain from the early 1840's **Sunday Schools** and **Temperance Organisations** and **employers** sponsored **trips** from **industrial cities** into the **countryside**.

Thomas Cook - Organised Temperance Excursions

One early pioneer, **Thomas Cook** a Baptist Lay Preacher who had signed the teetotal pledge in 1833, organised the first **temperance excursion** using the **railway** in **1846**. The 'special train' took 507 passengers 11 miles from Leicester to Loughborough. The trip included a Temperance prayer meeting and attendant festivities in a leafy park - a summer gala, band concert and cricket match - but strictly no alcohol. Cook went on to form The Thomas Cook Travel Agency which is still in existence today. His company Thomas Cook and Sons also exhibited their Travel Agency at the Royal Yorkshire Jubilee Exhibition at Saltaire in 1887 and advertised the Exhibition in local and national newspapers.

Regular Destination

Shipley Glen became a regular destination for Sunday School, Temperance and **Band of Hope** trips.

The Band of Hope was one of the great Victorian and Edwardian organizations, the first one being formed in **Leeds in 1847**. Many were associated with **Churches** and **temperance** classes and were often run in conjunction with **Sunday Schools**. Children were taught the temperance way of life and encouraged to sign the **teetotal pledge**. The Band of Hope targeted children of parents who wanted their children to be educated and have a secure future.

One of the **first Sunday School trips** made to the **Glen** was in **1853** when the Bradford Observer reported 200 children arriving from Halifax by rail. The trip and refreshments were provided by **Titus Salt** who accompanied the children to the Glen.

Temperance Hotels

Possibly anticipating the potential numbers who might be attracted to the area, Wood Head farm standing at the side of an old drovers road on Brackenhall Green was converted into the **Old Glen House and Hotel** by Charles Clegg in 1850. This small enterprise was believed to have been known as a **Temperance Hotel** which served afternoon teas to visitors. Charles Clegg retired in 1875.

The Old Glen House Temperance Hotel.

A second old building on the Green, built originally as an old **cruck house** was used by its owner Thomas Cooper to sell refreshments under the name of the **British Temperance Tea and Coffee House**. The *Leeds Times* of 23rd July, 1853 recorded:

"In the Glen there is an excellent house for refreshment known as the British Temperance Hotel and kept by Mr T. Cooper and has been occupied by him and his ancestors for over two centuries. It is a curious antique building supposed to be upwards of 400 years old, has no ceiling whilst the immense rafters and thatch are very prominent to the eye."

Essentially, a cruck house was a medieval house where the roof was supported by pairs of naturally curved timbers. This resulted in the roof having a built in curved shape.

The Bradford Observer of 4th February, 1875 also made comment about the building:

"There is in the Glen an old house called the British Temperance Hotel which is curious in itself and especially the interior, containing as it does as much oak as would make a small ship. The roof is formed like a charcoal burners stack."

British Temperance Tea and Coffee House.

British Temperance Tea and Coffee House.

Accommodation, Teas and Dancing

A further catering establishment was to be found on the Eldwick/ Bingley side of the Glen variously known as at New Scarboro on Sherrif Lane. It was called **Broadstones** or **The White House** and was run by Abraham Whitehead. First mention of the establishment was made in 1854 when advertisements stated that Sunday School Scholars could be accommodated. In 1857 dancing and games were advertised as being available. From 1881, William Denby a **Temperance House Keeper** is shown as running the business.

Growing Numbers of Visitors

Newspaper records show that by 1868 the Glen was becoming increasingly popular and busy, particularly at Easter, when working people from many parts of West Yorkshire flocked to the area.

At Easter 1869 it was reported that "thousands again repaired to Shipley Glen to spend the afternoon in various old English sports."

Broadstones/The White House.
Courtesy of Bingley and District Local History Society.

An Influx of Sunday - School Trips

June 1870 proved to be a busy time again for the Glen when it was reported that:

"A constant stream of visitors passed through Saltaire on their way to the Glen. From six in morning until six at night the stream never ceased.

On Monday afternoon the teachers and scholars of the Saltaire Congregational Church Sunday-school went to the Glen and were regaled with buns and tea. Then followed the Swedenborgians of Saltaire Sunday-schools on their way through the Glen to Gilstead where they had buns and tea and then joined in various old English sports. Then followed to the Glen the school teachers and scholars of the Primitive Methodists of Shipley in very large numbers and then the teachers and scholars of the Baptists of Shipley.

Tuesday had 3,000 visitors arriving by train from Leeds. Besides these there were thousands from other parts of the country."

COMMON LAND, BANK HOLIDAYS, MOORLAND RAMBLES AND FAIRS 1870 - 1880

With growing numbers now visiting the Glen, two pieces of legislation were to have an effect on the rights of those doing so. Both were intended to improve regular access to land which could provide public health benefits and relaxation in providing a breathing "lung" away from polluted manufacturing towns and cities.

Common Land Legislation

In 1865 The Commons Preservation Society (now the Open Spaces Society) was founded as a pressure group to help protect Common Land for the people. In 1870 a Bill for the Protection of Suburban Commons was brought to the House of Commons by MP, W. F. Cowper. The Bill sought to *"Exempt from enclosure, commons within five miles of a city or town of 5,000 inhabitants or within ten miles of a city or town of 30,000 inhabitants."*

The Bradford Observer of 5th January, 1870 reported:

*"The Bill for the Protection of Suburban Commons is of concern to **large towns** especially in **manufacturing districts** and of most concern to **working people** and poorer classes."*

It would however take a further five years until **Queen Victoria** would announce to Parliament:

*"My assent to the Bill for The Regulation and Improvement of Commons (**The Commons Act 1876**) and making amendments to Inclosure Acts to tend to the **preservation of open spaces** in the **neighbourhood** of **large towns** and to increase the **health** and comfort of my people."*

Subsequent legislation has sought to provide greater clarity to what is a very complex area. It is not the intention of this book to expand on or debate this topic, merely to highlight the existence of early legislation.

However, the effects of the Act directly on the Glen will be revisited on page 28 as regards Change of Ownership of Manorial Rights.

Bank Holiday Legislation

The second piece of legislation concerned workers holiday rights and entitlement.

In 1871 a Liberal MP, John Lubbock proposed the Bank Holidays Act. This was designed to ease the pressure on workers and shorten working hours by giving extra paid holidays on Easter Monday, Whit Monday the first Monday in August and Boxing Day. The immediate effect of this was to have significant effects for popular destinations such as the Glen as regards numbers visiting during these holidays.

Moorland Rambles

As early as 1869 the Bradford Observer had been extolling the virtues of walks on the moors. Their edition of 22nd June, 1869 carried the following report:

*"One of the greatest treats to the lovers of nature, who are pent up for the largest portion of their existence in the busy turmoil and **impure atmosphere of a large manufacturing town**, is to lay aside for a few hours the cares and troubles of business, to **sally forth to the moors** and enjoy the **bracing atmosphere** always to be found there.*

***Over the Moors to Ilkley** has a pleasant sound to the thousands of people who have crossed Rombalds Moor and have been gladdened by the bright prospects to be seen from this elevated region...*

One day last week business called us to Saltaire and after admiring the noble pile of almshouses, the handsome schools, the beautiful Independent chapel, the fine Methodist chapel the, baths and washouses and the comfortable houses which are growing up around this wonderful creation of Messrs Titus Salt, Sons and Co, we were tempted by the fresh north-west wind and clear atmosphere to traverse the moor to Ilkley...

Pausing at the Fleece Inn for rest and refreshment, before crossing the four miles of moor to Ilkley, Mr Hudson, the civil landlord informs us that he proposes to improve the pathway over the waste, which abounds in quagmires.

*Since the opening of the railway line to Ilkley, many people avail themselves of an **afternoon holiday walk** to that salubrious watering place and return home by evening train. A steep, narrow lane leads from the Fleece Inn onto the moor."*

Other Reasons for the Walk at Weekends?
Legislation
Alcohol could not be purchased in Britain on Sunday mornings (during divine services) from 1848 and opening hours on Sundays were reduced in 1854 and changed again in 1855.

These were among many proposals to ban all sales of alcohol in Britain on Sundays. However, those who had **travelled** more than **three miles** on a **Sunday** were permitted to purchase alcohol in pubs which had seven-day licences. This was known as Bona Fide Travellers legislation which was outlined in the Licensing Acts of 1872 and 1874.

A Local Context
Joe Hudson a family member and waiter at the Fleece (by then known affectionately as Dick Hudson's, after Richard the landlord) recalled that in 1882:

"Saltaire was just outside the three miles limit and at that time you could get a drink at any inn if you could prove that you had travelled three miles. The people of Saltaire made full use of this Act of Parliament on a Sunday.

We speak today of church-going and comparison is made of the good old days when people went to church or chapel, ...well, I can speak of this period 70 years ago, when on a fine summers day, especially, many could be seen making their way over Shipley Glen to Dick's who should perhaps have been at some place of worship.

I can speak or write with authority because it was my duty to enquire of each customer... "How far have you come and where do you come from?"

Yorkshire Rambles
Commencing in 1873 local newspapers further profiled **walks** from **Saltaire** via the **Glen** over **Rombalds Moor** to **Ilkley** generally under the title Yorkshire Rambles. The distance to Ilkley was **seven miles** and

walkers could either return back over the moor or alternatively catch the train from Ilkley to Leeds or Bradford.

These walks were undertaken by growing numbers of people, some of whom took the opportunity to visit public houses such as the Glen at Gilstead (run by dialect poet Ben Preston), or the Acorn at Eldwick or at **Dick Hudson's**. The latter was renowned for the quality of its home cured and produced ham and egg lunches. (See photographs below.)

Acorn Inn, Eldwick.

Dick Hudson's.
    Courtesy of Bingley and District Local History Society.

Increasing Numbers

Possibly stimulated by the extra Bank Holidays the number of visitors to the Glen increased radically from 1872, particularly at Easter. In that year eight special trains were laid on by the Midland railway to transport additional passengers to the Glen.

This occurred again in **1873** when special trains were again laid on to transport an estimated **15 to 20,000** visitors to the Glen. By **1874** this had increased to **35,000** no doubt due to the introduction of **fairground attractions** onto the Glen.

Fairground Legislation

The National Fairground and Circus Archive at the University of Sheffield (2018) identifies:

*"Fairs throughout the country seemed in danger in the 1860s and 1870s, not only as a result of The Fairs Acts of 1868, 1871, and 1873, but also because of the **loss of traditional sites in town centres.**"*

However the Glen as a **vast area of open space** offered a perfect solution to this problem. Historian Thomas Frost writing in 1874 believed that fairs had become unnecessary when he stated:

"Fairs are becoming extinct The nation has outgrown them, and fairs are as dead as the generations which they have delighted, and the last showman will soon be as great a curiosity as the dodo."

Despite this prophecy fairs continued to survive and flourish, particularly on the Glen.

The First Fair on the Glen

Whilst some of the Temperance Houses had previously laid on galas in their grounds featuring swings, games, brass band music and occasionally dancing, other forms of entertainment were not at that stage offered.

That was until the first Fair or nearer to the truth...gathering of opportunist and itinerant showmen offering a variety of entertainment choices, at **Easter 1873**.

These included merry-go-rounds, archery, games of choice, quoits and "Aunt Sally" stalls. Such holiday fairs would expand and become a feature of what was offered on the Glen for the **next forty years**. The last fair (before mechanical roundabouts were excluded) was held at Easter 1913 and attracted an estimated 100,000 people!

New Lord of the Manor

Initially there was no charge to the showmen for erecting their stalls and amusements on the Glen. However, in 1876, on the death of his father, **Colonel William Wade Maude** succeeded to the title of **Lord of the Manor of Baildon**.

On 20th April 1878 the Bradford Observer reported that Maude had issued a cautionary notice regarding trespass by any showmen who erected stalls on the Glen. Amongst other things this stated:

"Hitherto no charge has been made for the privilege of placing stalls and the usual appurtenances of a fair upon the ground and it was simply in order to establish his claim for the tollage that the Lord of the Manor caused a cautionary trespass notice to be circulated...

*Yesterday the ground was well covered and occupied by the temporary stands of showmen and refreshment dealers. For each itinerant proprietor, **a charge** proportionate to the pretentions of their establishment was made and except in a few instances payment was made without grumbling...*

*Grand galas were held in adjoining fields and establishments for which special bands were engaged and altogether the Glen was a busy scene...*The next year - **1879** proved to be the most successful Easter to date with **45/50,000** visitors!

Courtesy of Bingley and District Local History Society.

TEMPERANCE HOTELS - CHANGES ON THE GLEN 1881 - 1886

Old Glen House

Contrary to previous published research regarding John Pickles Dewhirst taking over the Old Glen House on the retirement of Charles Clegg in 1875... the following was the case:

The Bradford Observer advertised the sale of the premises on 16th July 1879 as follows:

"To be Sold at the well known and highly popular resort known as Shipley Glen, the old established GLEN HOUSE and Refreshment Rooms containing five rooms on the ground floor, with cellaring and out kitchen, nine bed-rooms, also a large refreshment and concert room and cloak-room with gardens and conveniences.

The present and prospective advantages of this property are considerable and well worth the attention of anyone intending to enter the refreshment and lodging house business."

By May 1880 Dewhirst was advertising the Old Glen House as a Tea and Strawberry Garden, not as a Temperance establishment as such. However he appears to be keeping his options open by entertaining the Bradford Band of Hope and Temperance Society for tea in July 1881.

Interestingly, a month later his application for a licence to sell alcohol at the Old Glen was heard by the Otley Brewster Sessions and opposed by the Solicitor for the Baildon Temperance Society. Mr Dewhirst contended that there were no public houses in Saltaire and that the nearest public house where visitors could get a drink was in Eldwick. The licence was however not granted.

Mr Edward Salt one of the sons of Sir Titus Salt who attended the sessions pointed out that although there were no licensed premises on the Glen the numbers of visitors were increasing each year.

During 1882 and 1883 Mr Dewhirst advertised frequently that at the entrance to the Glen **Circular Tram Cars** were running at the Old Glen and additionally that there was a large room with a seating capacity of 300 at the establishment. He also built boat-swings and gave donkey rides in the garden, which his own three children, who were all born at the Old Glen between 1881 and 1887 enjoyed using.

Childhood Memories

The following account was written by Annie Florence Eastell looking back at her childhood on the Glen. It was written possibly in the early 1950's as a retrospective view of her youth.

"I was born in 1887 at the Old Glen House, the youngest daughter of the late Mr and Mrs J P Dewhirst. My parents were owners of the Old Glen House from 1880 when it was purchased by my grandfather, until 1909 when my father died.

From my earliest years I helped my parents in the business of providing meals and refreshments at the establishment. I understand that such business was conducted on the premises prior to my parents occupation.

The business involved the preparation on a paraffin stove (there were no gas or electricity supplies to the Glen in those days) *of both full meals, including ham and eggs, which were served on the premises throughout the day; and also afternoon teas and pots of tea which were consumed both in the house, the adjacent tea room, and in the gardens.*

Some of the customers were local workmen, but the majority were people on outings, particularly at weekends and holidays who were visiting the many attractions and entertainment on Shipley Glen, including the Glen Tramway. At holiday times, in particular on Easter Monday, many thousands of people would visit the Glen and we were kept very busy at such times.

In addition to being involved in my parents catering business, I also helped my mother make lemon cheese, which as J P Dewhirsts Lemon Cheese became famous at the turn of the century. When my father died the catering business was sold as a going concern.

Having myself continued to live in the area ever since 1909 I know that the use of the Old Glen House as a restaurant and cafe and tea room has continued unabated through two world wars, up until the present day."

Postscript

As pointed out above James Pickles Dewhirst died at Old Glen house in 1909 having been resident there for 29 years. Varo (1984 pp30) identifies that up until 1918 the catering business was continued by Herbert and Elizabeth Badland, then Thomas and Jane Midgley ran the establishment until 1946. From 1947, Madge Raistrick operated the business as a restaurant, cafe and tearoom, and also bred peacocks there. She retired in 1983.

The Old Cruck House and Temperance Hotel

This building was demolished in 1885 when the Lord of the Manor insisted that the Cooper family leave the building. Initially a wooden hut was built in the garden to provide catering. The Cooper family appear to have continued to provide afternoon garden teas there. Part of this site is now the Bracken Hall Countryside Centre which is currently run by volunteers.

Courtesy of Bingley & District Local History Society.

Postscript

Thomas and Hannah Cooper are reputed to be the first people to have provided ham and egg teas for visitors to the Glen. They kept a pig, hens, bees and a large garden well stocked with birds and fruit. Tom was well known locally as a herbalist whom people came to for medicines. They also produced Old Glen Toffee. Tom Died in 1887 and Hannah died in 1888.

After the Cruck House was demolished the Cooper family eventually built a new house on Prod Lane which they called Coopers Tea Gardens. These were run by Mary Ann Cooper. Coopers Tea Gardens, Board, Residence and Apartments plus Glen Toffee were all advertised locally between 1913 and 1916.

The Last Year of Temperance Activity

Trips to the Glen organised by temperance inspired movements lasted for over 25 years. The last recorded large temperance visits to the Glen were made by the Girlington Band of Hope and the Bradford Band of Hope in July and August 1888.

Transport

To facilitate greater mobility locally and to augment existing rail connections, Bradford introduced trams progressively over the next twenty years. Initially these were organised by the Bradford Tramway and Omnibus Company. In 1882 the first horse drawn trams were introduced and were complemented by steam trams in 1883. By 1898 Bradford Corporation had assumed responsibility and implemented the first electric trams. Increasing numbers of visitors would utilise these and a range of horse drawn wagonettes and charabancs to reach the Glen, depending on which they could best afford.

The Next Stage of Development on the Glen

Now, however to **transport** and **rides** of a **different nature**. The next stage of development involved a **transition** from **gentle**, more **traditional forms** of Victorian entertainment which had previously been part of the Glen experience, towards more **adventurous** experiences and **thrills**.

Realising that people seemed to enjoy being thrown about and jostled and that money could be made from outdoor thrill rides, the race was on to create experiences which would attract the biggest crowds.

Such an approach would be developed towards the close of the century at such venues as Coney Island, New York and at Blackpool.

The stimulus for local change of this nature, which eventually impacted on the Glen, was the Royal Yorkshire Jubilee Exhibition held at Saltaire in 1887. The Exhibition offered several such thrill rides and experiences which people could try for the first time and which are described in the next section.

SALTAIRE EXHIBITION AS THE MODEL FOR DEVELOPING SHIPLEY GLEN RIDES - 1887

In October 1886 Titus Salt Junior proposed a memorial event for his father by building a new School of Art and Science in Saltaire. The original Schools, housed as an Institute in the Victoria Hall had proved to be such a success that by the date of the proposal, they needed more space.

It was therefore suggested that a new School be built behind the existing building. It was also simultaneously proposed that an **International Exhibition** should be held to celebrate **the Jubilee** of **Queen Victoria** in **1887**.

The Royal Yorkshire Jubilee Exhibition was opened by Princess Beatrice, the youngest daughter of Queen Victoria on 6th May, 1887.

Buildings

Amongst the buildings constructed for the Exhibition were a Concert Hall seating 3,000 people and a covered avenue with themed Exhibition Courts along its length. There were also Art Galleries, Refreshment bars, a Temperance Cafe and a photographers studio. The Yorkshire Post and Intelligencer of 16th of October 1886 described the provision:

"In a very roomy hall, concerts and other events will take place and the dining and refreshment rooms are to be remarkably complete."

The article then describes the objective of the Exhibition as profiling British and International industry and commerce, art and education whilst also using proceeds to raise funds for the building of the new school. Entertainment facilities were also described:

*"About six acres of land will be elaborately laid out in **pleasure grounds** and gardens with promenades - open and canopied, fountains, grottoes, shrubberies and all manner of **pleasure-yielding surroundings**."*

Pleasure Grounds

The plan (below) published in the Leeds Mercury in 1886 shows these outdoor spaces which also contained gardens, a maze, a bandstand, a Camera Obscura, a Toboggan Slide and a Japanese Village. Not shown on the plan, but later described in newspapers as being situated near the Toboggan Slide was a Switchback Railway.

Some of these would have a direct effect on the next development of the Glen as an area offering "thrill" rides, whilst others like the camera obscura would offer more passive entertainment.

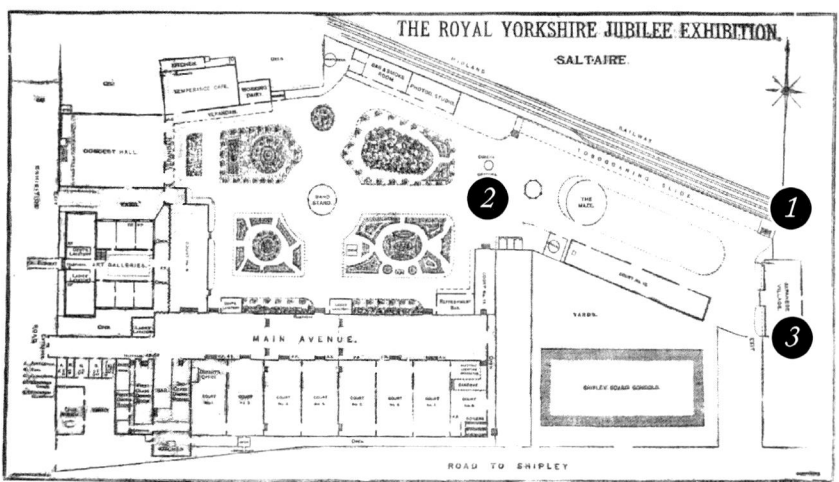

1: Toboggan Slide. 2: Camera Obscura. 3: Japanese Village.
Courtesy of Shipley College, Saltaire Archives.

Pleasure Ground Preview

At Easter 1887 the Bradford Daily Telegraph of 12th April made the following important **link** between the **Glen** and the **Exhibition**:

"On Good Friday the Glen, as usual was the favourite place of resort, but for the first time yesterday the grounds of the Royal Yorkshire Jubilee Exhibition were open to the public. A good number of people availed themselves of this opportunity to get a glimpse of the Exhibition and during the afternoon the grounds were crowded. The refreshment bar was open and the toboggan slide under the management of Messrs Brown and Backhouse was running."

Summary of the background to Pleasure Ground entertainment at the Exhibition:

The Camera Obscura - (The workings of which are described on page 41) was a rotating viewing chamber which used a pinhole camera principle to project an image of outside surroundings onto a table in front of the people viewing it. The first purpose built and oldest Victorian camera obscura was set up in Edinburgh by optician Maria Short in 1853 and is still in operation.

The Toboggan Slide - Originally a snow orientated pastime in Canada, tobogganing on a wooden track had been adapted for fairground and pleasure ground purposes in a number of countries. By 1887 plans and licences were being sold by the United Kingdom Tobogganing Company in Britain. Saltaire was granted one such licence by the company. Actual installation was carried out by Brown and Backhouse of Liverpool. The ride was 370 feet in length and ran on four tracks. Each of the dozen cars carried up to four passengers.

The Ocean Wave Switchback - Was installed to the plans of Bainbridge and Bapty of Manchester in June 1887 as a late addition to the pleasure grounds. The run was 440 feet in length and was described as exhilarating and novel. It was reported that the ride had averaged 3,000 passengers per day between June and September 1887.

The Japanese Village

Between 1885 and 1887 a Japanese Village was built in Knightsbridge, London to resemble a traditional Japanese community. This exhibition was a commercial venture organised by Tannaker Buhicrosan, who had been organising travelling Japanese exhibitions in Britain for several years beforehand.

Tannakers Japanese Village was also a feature of the Saltaire Exhibition and was in all probability the stimulus and inspiration for Thomas Hartley building his Japanese Gardens on Shipley Glen. Hartley went to live on Prod Lane, in 1886.

Dismantling of the Exhibition and Pleasure Grounds

The Exhibition closed on 29th October, 1887, the registered turnstile figures showing that 809,350 people had visited it.

Some of the buildings were put up for sale including the Concert Hall and Pavilions which were bought for re erection at a pleasure ground in Douglas, Isle of Man. The Leeds Times of 19th November noted that the toboggan slide and Japanese Village had "disappeared" and the switchback railway was following them into retirement.

Local Interest

However, newspaper records show that the **switchback** was bought locally and re erected on Shipley Glen. It had originally cost the exhibition authorities £500 and was bought for £100.

Additionally, a Camera Obscura used at the Exhibition was also advertised for sale.

The next chapter and sections detail the background and workings of each of the new attractions on the Glen and the dates that they were introduced.

THE RIDES - 1888 - 1898

The Switchback - 1888

Re-siting on the Glen

In March 1888 the Leeds Mercury reported that the Switchback had been transferred from the Saltaire Exhibition Grounds to the Shipley Glen Plateau by local amusement speculators. They had paid £100 to re-site it in a field next to the barn at Brackenhall Farm. The speculators were not identified, but there is evidence that the sale was made by C E Taylor Auctioneers privately and not as part of the equipment sold off from effects of the Royal Yorkshire Jubilee Exhibition.

The Ride

The ride, renamed The Royal Yorkshire Switchback was built of pitch pine and redwood. The Wharfedale and Airedale Observer described it as follows:

"The Switchback is an extension of the toboggan... The toboggan is what may be described as the elementary and the switchback as the advanced stage of this amusement which has come to us from across the Atlantic.

Riding on it is best described as like sailing over large billows at a rapid rate, or like tobogganing intensified. The journey is made on cars, each capable of seating ten persons and by means of tracks, outward and return journeys are made.

The tracks consist of two narrow gauge lines of rails laid upon a wooden platform, fixed upon wooden supports of great length at each end of the track and varying between the two extremities, affording gradients sufficiently steep to allow the cars to traverse the whole length of the ride at speed.

*As the occupants plunge down the slopes and rush up the corresponding inclines the sensation is of **pleasurable excitement**. The cars are lightly built of wood and are fitted with a brake that is applied automatically when the journey is completed. They are three in number...At the rate of transit it is estimated that nearly a mile could be traversed in about 50 seconds."*

Excitement

One early trip to the Switchback was made by 120 employees from Brown's Wholesale Clothiers of Hebden Bridge whose day out to the Glen was highlighted by their **excitement** of experiencing the Switchback ride.

Danger

However whilst patrons may have been excited, a Bradford Daily Telegraph report in August 1888 warned:

"The rage for something new in the way of amusement has added fresh terrors to local fairs and wakes. These we have in the "switchback" and other similar institutions and this week we have had a couple of illustrations of the damage these new inventions can achieve."

The article then mentions and describes two local switchback accidents, one at Shipley fair (not the Glen Switchback) and the other at Dewsbury, and ends:

"It is within the province we believe of local authorities to prohibit any form of amusement which they have reason to consider is dangerous. This new instrument of destruction surely merits attention."

In the event, the Royal Yorkshire Switchback was to have an excellent safety record up until it was auctioned, sold for £99 and removed by John Smith, a Scrap Metal Dealer in 1917.

However, as described in following sections, the **Aerial Flight** and the **Toboggan** ride, two **later Glen attractions**, although highly popular, were questioned as being **unsafe** by Bradford Corporation and were **eventually withdrawn** from service.

The Aerial Flight is covered in detail on pages 42 - 47 and it is the least known and researched Glen ride. There were also a number of controversial issues associated with it which are also covered in detail and put into context.

The Horse Drawn Tram - 1888

Sam Wilson, a publican, (who was eventually involved in installing a number of rides on the Glen) and a business partner, are rumoured to have bought six horse drawn open toast rack cars which had been used at the Jubilee Exhibition.

Courtesy of The Glen Tramway.

Two of these, capable of seating up to 20 people, were said to have been sited on the Glen and used to circle the now defunct Glen Pond situated near to the Old Glen House. This may have been an addition to the Shipley Glen Tram Cars advertised by the Old Glen in 1883. Varo (1985 pp27) mentions:

"...a railtrack laid around a circular pond at the bottom of the garden, a horse drawn four wheeled bogey being used to give pleasure rides to its eager patrons."

The remaining four toast rack cars were reputed to have been stored for later use on the Glen Tramway, built in 1895.

Camera Obscura - 1888

In December 1887 an advertisement appeared in the Leeds Mercury announcing an auction of some of the effects of the Jubilee Exhibition including: *"one camera obscura with lens, all complete and in excellent condition, only been in use six months."*

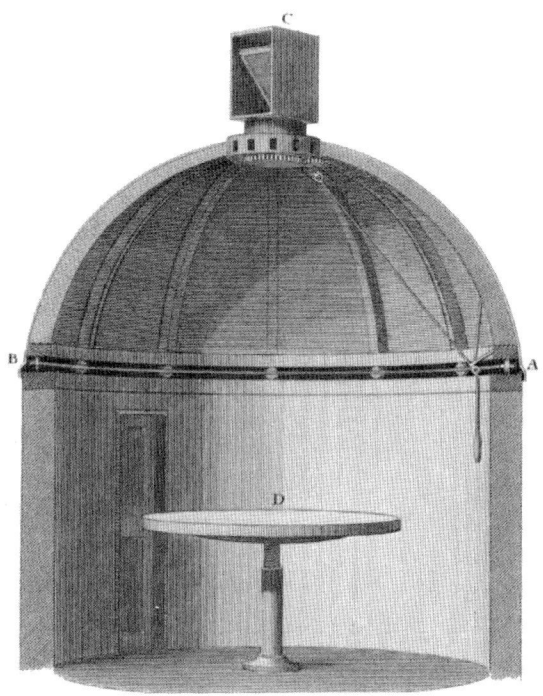

It is highly probable that by early 1888 this had been purchased as one of **two giant camera obscuras** introduced as attractions to the Glen. The first Obscura was located in the same field as the Switchback, close to Brackenhall Farm.

For a small charge, a 360 degree view of the surrounding area could be viewed from inside the darkened hut which housed the obscura. A series of mirrors and prisms placed at the highest point of the roof (**C**) reflected light down through a lens below and onto a viewing table (**D**). The 360 degree view could be obtained by rotating the roof of the hut which ran on bearings, by handle (**A**) and (**B**) (see previous page).

Other attractions on the Glen were however less passive.

The Aerial Flight - 1889

Ariel Flight Patents

The first Aerial Flight rides in England were patented by J. W. Stansfield of Todmorden and built and operated at Blackpool and Southport in 1887 and 1888.

THE START

IN MID-COURSE

The Pall Mall Gazette described the Blackpool ride as:

"The world's first cable car ride, the Aerial Flight will become a rival to the switchback and toboggan. It is expected to eclipse both the older varieties of swift locomotion and as the cars glide through the air on wire ropes it affords the additional sensation of ballooning."

Accident

Unfortunately on 11th September, 1888 one of the fastenings supporting the ropes on the Blackpool ride became detached and seven people were injured when the wooden gondola in which they were travelling hit a wall. The accident was widely reported in newspapers nationally.

The Glen Aerial Flight

Local men Badland and Halliday built the Aerial Flight on the escarpment at the top of the Glen in 1889. It would appear likely that they had knowledge of Stansfield's patent. Sam Halliday and his sons were blacksmiths and may well have adapted and built the Glen version of the Flight.

Courtesy of Dorothy Burrows.

Initially feelings about the construction ran high locally as an article in the Leeds Mercury in March 1889 headed **Alleged Vandalism in Shipley Glen** demonstrates:

*"No little commotion has been caused to the people who reside in the neighbourhoods of Baildon, Shipley and Saltaire by the appearance above the trees of a **huge wooden skeleton** which is to be utilised by speculators who hope to make money from thousands of holiday-makers who visit the Glen.*

*Something like a year ago the **switchback railroad** was erected in a field on the plateau at the top of the Glen which had previously done duty at the Saltaire Exhibition, and this is certainly no improvement to the natural scenery, but the structure now being put up is something more offensive.*

*Instead of being fixed as much out of the general view as possible it holds the most prominent position overlooking the valley and is erected on what has **always been considered common ground** to which everybody has a right. It appears that fired by the success of the switchback venture, a company called the Aerial Flight Company has been formed."*

Controversy

Before the Easter holidays in 1889 had even started, a far reaching debate concerning the Glen had occupied the pages of local and regional newspapers. This concerned three aspects, namely:

- Colonel Maude's wish to exercise his **legal rights as Lord of the Manor** including the jurisdiction of a group named the Amalgated Company of Showmen and Amusement Caterers to levy tolls on the Glen. Additionally, questions were asked regarding the building of a permanent structure on what was believed to be "**common ground**."

- The formation of the Aerial Flight Company and their proposal to build the Aerial Flight at the top of the Glen. Concerns about the **safety** of the proposed ride were also expressed.

- The "defacement" of the Glen by the building of the Aerial Flight, which was deemed to be **unsightly**.

The Amalgamated Company of Showmen and Amusement Caterers

The Shipley Times and Express reported in April that the company consisted of a number of enterprising capitalists whose headquarters were in Bradford. Apparently, Colonel Maude, the Lord of the Manor had granted them the right to let off portions of Baildon Moor and the Glen to showmen and caterers at Easter and Whitsuntide.

Questions were raised as to what that might entail in the long term as regards public access to the Glen. Additionally, concerns were expressed as to destroying the natural beauty of the Glen as a destination for thousands of working people.

"Common Land"

The Ilkley Gazette and Wharfedale Advertiser of 23rd March, 1889 made the following comment:

"The amusement caterers and stallholders who go to the plateau of Shipley Glen during Spring and Summer, pay a toll to the Lord of the Manor, but whether he has the right to let off for a permanent structure a portion of what is believed to be "common land" remains to be seen.

The Bradford Branch of the Commons Preservation Society have been asked to take the matter up. Several members of the Society have visited the spot for the purpose of making a report to their headquarters and every effort will be made to prevent the infringement of public privilege and right."

Colonel Maude's solicitors response to matters concerning common land and to suggestions made by Bradford Corporation that maybe the Glen and the public might be better served by the creation of a public park were as follows:

"Referring to your suggestion as to the future appropriation of some portion of Baildon Moor Glen for a public park or recreation ground, Colonel Maude will be prepared to receive in friendly spirit any proposal from the Corporation with that object and would suggest that if the Corporation are earnest in the matter, they should at once put themselves in communication with us.

The settlement of that illimitable question of **common rights** *and the difficulty of either the municipality of Bradford or any other body, private or public, arranging with the Lord of the Manor as to future control of the Glen, would call for an* **intervention of Parliament.***"*

The Aerial Flight Company

The members of the Aerial Flight Company were declared as being William Wade Maude, A. Halliday, Mark Badland (Secretary) Alderman Walbank, John Bell, John Bradley and William Tyson.

During early April the Corporation of Bradford through its Town Clerk had been in "friendly" correspondence with the solicitors of the Lord of the Manor. The Solicitors had stated that Colonel Maude could not at this late stage put a stop to operations as the proprietors of the Flight had spent a large sum in catering for public amusement during Easter.

As regards **danger to the public** who may use the Flight, Colonel Maude had been assured by the proprietors that every care would be taken to test its stability and that similar erections had been greatly used at **Southport** and **Blackpool** and other places **without accident**. This was not the case.

The proprietors had stated that when the apparatus was completed they had further undertaken to have it carefully examined and certified by local engineer of note. In the event Mr W. B. Woodhead, Chartered Engineer made a **test of the ropes and cars** and declared them **safe**.

Safety and Unsightliness

The Craven Herald reported on 27th April, 1889:

"At Otley Police Court, Superintendant Harrison intimated that he had inspected the Aerial Flight at Shipley Glen and reported "Although an eyesore and damaging to the natural beauties of the place, it is not more so than the host of shooting galleries, boxing booths and other caterings of folly which periodically gather there."

The chief reasons advanced in the notice from the Town Clerks office in Bradford recently for its removal are, its dangerous character, its being an obstruction to the public frequenting the Glen and, its being a nuisance.

*There is an **element of danger** in many of these erections but on this, **every precaution** seems to have been taken to reduce it to a **minimum**...There is no **obstruction**...and I am unable to see how it can be brought under the **Act for the Suppression of Public Nuisances**. The erection is authorised by the Lord of the Manor and he believes that he is within his legal rights. The case is therefore one for the Higher Courts."*

The Aerial Flight was opened over Easter 1889 and achieved immediate success. The Wharfedale and Airedale Observer of 27th April commented:

*"The once popular **switchback** was **overshadowed** by the much maligned*

Aerial Flight which was extensively patronised from noon, until darkness prevented further business."

The Ride

The same newspaper commented on the ride as follows:

The flight is an ingenious arrangement for testing the nerves though the sensation is hardly so exhilarating as that of the switchback.

The passengers mount stairs leading to a covered platform, at a height of between 33 and 40 feet to take their seats in a gondola car, capable of seating eight persons, which is shoved into space by a couple of stalwart men. The car glides through the air suspended from two grooved wheels that run along a stout steel wire cable. The cable is stretched to a slightly lower platform (the gradient between the higher and lower platform being 10 feet) more than 200 yards distant and the impetus given at the start is sufficient to land the delighted or otherwise, occupants.

Attached to the upper fitting of each car is a smaller wire rope which is on an endless principle, so the force of the loaded car serves to return the empty vehicle."

Courtesy of Bill Slessor.

The Opening of the Aerial Flight

The publicity achieved by virtue of the controversy previously outlined, ensured a busy first appearance of the ride.

The Shipley Times and Express coverage of 27th April captured the scale of this:

"The principle feature of the Easter holidays on Shipley Glen was the tremendously advertised Aerial Flight. The company of speculators who have come to terms with the Lord of the Manor for the erection of this structure ought to be extremely grateful to those people who have thought it their duty to protest about the defacement of natural scenery which has taken place.

*While the protest may bear fruit in the future in securing advantages for the general public, its immediate effect was to bring an **immense number** of **curious people** to Shipley Glen. The visitors to the Glen apparently cared nothing for the desecration which had taken place and evidently were prepared to **adopt the new plaything** as a godsend, after other attractions had grown stale.*

At any rate, the aerial did a brisk trade throughout the afternoon, probably something like 3,000 passengers entering the cars up until 8pm when the box closed."

However - An Accident!

The same newspaper article continued its coverage...

"There was not that immunity from accident which the promoters of the aerial had predicted and which Superintendant Harrison of Otley rather too readily assumed, though strictly speaking the accident that happened was not due to any structural defect."

Laura Shaw of Bradford was apparently excitedly waiting on the platform to enter a gondola car when she stepped too near the edge. She caught hold of one of the steel wires just after it had set in motion...

"She was drawn over the edge of the platform and fell to the ground. The consternation of the people at what had happened was very great and it was generally expected that she would be killed or injured. Happily it was neither one nor the other.

There was a strongish wind blowing and doubtless the effect of the wind in *her clothing prevented her falling with violence – in fact it was an **accidental parachute performance**. In her descent she turned a somersault and came to the ground fortunately on a piece of turf, on her side, between two rocks.*

She was unconscious when taken up and was conveyed to an adjoining farmhouse (Mr Walker's) where she recovered consciousness."

Although taken home by cab she was admitted next day for a short stay in Bradford Hospital suffering from shock and bruising.

Despite this first accident, the **Aerial Flight** was to prove to be one of the **safer** rides on the Glen until it was **closed** in **1901** on the recommendation of **Bradford Corporation**.

Before that however, the next year (1890) heralded the start of changes which would eventually affect the entertainment opportunities on the Glen.

Precursors to Change – 1890

After the introduction of the Aerial Flight in 1889, the following year and particularly Easter 1890, proved to be eventful for patrons of the Glen. So much so, that the Shipley Times and Express reported that there had been 20,000 visitors on Good Friday alone and that there had been *"a continuous stream of people up and down the Glen from noon until late at night."*

It was also reported that the Switchback and Aerial Flight did *"brisk business."*

Several actions and circumstances which would have more long term effects on the nature of the Glen can be attributed to changes which occurred in 1890.

Commons Preservation

In April the Shipley Times and Express reported:

*"So far the agitation started last summer by the **Commons Preservation Society**, for securing the **public rights** for the Glen have resulted in less than nothing; for if possible the Manorial Rights are riveted stronger than ever, and as the as the Aerial Flight and Switchback railway have proved*

themselves to be profit making undertakings, the Baildon shareholders in those concerns are not likely to relinquish their position...

*The Switchback is located in a field adjoining the plateau and is **not** a matter of **common rights**....but the Aerial Flight is controlled by a company who have a lease from the Lord of the Manor."*

Rent Collection

The same newspaper reported that in 1889 the Lord of the Manor had let off rights to a company of amusement caterers for the use of the Glen plateau. However in the current year (1890) the **Manor Bailiff**, Jeremiah Garnett would be **letting** off the ground to **itinerant showmen** who would convert the area into a *"perfect fairground."* Such rents received from stallholders and showmen were expected to exceed those of the year before.

Comment was also made that whilst there was opportunity for *"rowdy amusement,"* those who enjoyed the area for the peace of nature would be thankful that the fair only occurred once or twice a year!

Intoxicating Liquor

For four days over the Easter holidays, and for the **first time** since the Glen became popular, **intoxicating drinks** were sold. A temporary licence was granted by Otley magistrates to a refreshment caterer from Bradford who had rented a field adjoining the Glen common.

The Shipley Times and Express reported:

*"As the Bingley magistrates have repeatedly refused similar applications from Glen refreshment house keepers, who reside permanently at the place, the action of the Otley Bench was viewed with some indignation, not only by **teetotallers** but by the people of the district who feel that the **concession** should have been made, if at all, to a **local resident**. There had been no complaint of drunkenness, but it is quite certain that strong opposition will be offered to the granting of a licence at any future time."*

The next ten years would herald a number of changes on the Glen including a Transfer of Manorial Rights and the introduction of **two new rides**.

The Glen Tramway - 1895

The first of these new rides was the Glen Tramway.

This section covers the initial building of the Tramway and its opening in 1895.

The full history of the Tramway was published in Leak M.J (2003) *100 Years at Shipley Glen - The Story of the Glen Tramway* and subsequently updated in 2016 (see Bibliography). This can be purchased from the upper or lower stations of the Tramway.

Access to the Glen

The Glen Tramway built in late 1894/early 1895 by local man Sam Wilson and his business partner Mr H. Wilkinson, was intended to provide an **alternative** to the **steep path** to the Glen plateau.

Whilst little is known about Mr Wilkinson, the Yorkshire Evening Post of 16th August 1917 later identified him as a Foreman Delver (Quarryman) who Sam Wilson *"had engaged to remove the rocks in the line of the track."* They seemingly remained business partners for ten years.

It goes without saying that a number of concerned locals voiced their opinions regarding; the **defacement** of the side of the Glen; the "**scar**" that it left down the side of the valley and; the **unsightly nature** of the black fencing posts which separated the footpath and the tramway, for safety reasons.

Plans

Initial plans drawn up by Sam Wilson for a "wire rope railway" from Walker Wood near Saltaire Park to Shipley Glen were submitted to the Baildon Local Board for approval in late November 1894.

The Shipley Times and Express announced on 1st December 1894 that the plans had been provisionally approved and that work would start immediately as the **ground rent** being charged by the Lord of the Manor who owned the wood, was **already in operation**:

The Proposed Railway up Shipley Glen Wood
The Plans Passed and Work Commenced

Sam Wilson.   Courtesy of Shipley Glen Tramway.

"As briefly reported last week, a railway up Walker Wood commonly known as Glen Wood , Saltaire, will shortly be accomplished in fact. The Baildon Local Board has **provisionally passed plans** and the Lord of the Manor (Colonel W W Maude) has this week entered into an arrangement with the promoter of the passenger railway – Mr Samuel Wilson, late landlord of the Malt Shovel Inn, Baildon, so that nothing now remains but to carry out the work, which will be done with **all possible speed** as the **ground rent** is **already in operation.**

The length of the line already settled upon will be 500 yards and will commence at the bottom of Glen Wood, where the present footpath enters the wood. The line will be of a **gradient** of **one in nine**, the gauge will be **twenty inches**, there will be **two sets of rails** and the upper terminus of the railway will be at the top of the woods near the Prod Lane gate, where the footpath turns to the right in the direction of Baildon.

Here an engine-house will be built, and will probably contain an oil engine, the Shipley Gas Company having refused to convey gas there, but the Saltaire Syndicate may consent to do so, though that is not settled – in which case a gas engine will be the motive power. In the triangular plantation at the top of Walker Wood, Mr Wilson intends to build himself a dwelling house and the engine-house will be of corrugated zinc.

*The **railway** will be constructed in a **straight line** on the upper side of the present footpath and for some distance will run parallel with the footpath, but at a point lower down the railway will pass further into the wood, leaving the footpath on the right and coming out again at the end of the lane leading to the Carriage Drive.*

*The cars will be worked by an **endless wire rope** and a patent apparatus belonging to Mr Wilson and Mr Hardcastle of Manningham for clamping and unclamping the rope, will be attached to the cars in addition to two safety brakes (patented by Messrs Wilson and Hardcastle), which immediately come into action automatically in case a car becomes disconnected by accident and thus bringing the car to a stand, the principal end in view being the safety of the public.*

Each car will accommodate twelve passengers on six seats and the cars will be open air after the style of the switchback cars, but improved. The cars will run up level, the hind wheel being nine inches higher than those in front, similar to the hydraulic tramways in Scarborough. Landing stages will be erected at either end of the line, and when in operation it will employ six persons. The present footpath will not be interfered with, but the railway will be fenced from top to bottom.

The estimated cost of the present section is £500, but if arrangements can be made with the fields abutting upon the Carriage Drive (Sir Titus Salt, Bart, Sons and Co), the railway will be carried diagonally across the field situated between the present lane leading from this road into the wood and that leading towards Baildon Green, and in that case the lower terminus of the line will be at the corner of Saltaire Park and immediately facing Saltaire Bridge. If the Saltaire Firm consent to this field being used for such a purpose – and we believe one member of the firm favourably entertains the proposal – the cost of the railway will be about £700. If not, however the railway will stop at the bottom of Glen Wood.

Courtesy of Shipley Glen Tramway.

The line has already been marked out, and will be proceeded with at once, under Mr Wilson's supervision and will be in working order before Easter - sooner if possible."

Delayed Opening

Unfortunately the opening was delayed when it was discovered that the rope-pulleys were too small and the speed attained by the cars was too fast, namely twenty miles per hour rather than the safer speed required of ten miles per hour. Consequently for reasons of safety, Wilson and Wilkinson, advised by Mr John Waugh a Civil Engineer, postponed the opening until May to allow for the necessary alterations to be carried out. The official inspection was made by Mr Waugh on 17th May and the tramway opened the next day.

Shorter Track

After unsuccessful negotiations with the new owners of Salts Estates, Sir James Roberts, the length of the track was reduced from 500 yards to 440 yards. (A survey carried out by a local engineering firm in 1937 measured the track at exactly 386 yards).

Different Motive Power

In the event the initial motive power installed was *"gas, obtained from one of John Robson's eight horse power Shipley Gas Engines."* The gas used initially was producer gas, produced on site by burning anthracite coal, the gas having a distinctive and rather unpleasant smell.

Leak (2003) reports that before the end of the 19th Century a deal had been done with Salts Mill to supply town gas from their gas holder. A newspaper report confirms *"the gas being obtained through a pipe laid from Saltaire"* originally laid by Mr H. Firth of Shipley.

Postscript

The Robson engine ran on various fuels - from gas to oil over its 34 year existence. In 1929 the new owner of the Tramway decided to convert to electricity.

Technical Specifications

The new rope pulleys designed to reduce the working speed to 10mph were supplied by the Unbreakable Pulley Company of Manchester and fixed by Mr Brearley of Shipley.

The cars were designed to be carried along by means of a securely clamped crucible steel **rope five eighths of an inch thick**, the **breaking strain** of which was warranted by the makers, Messrs Craddock to be **fourteen and a half tons**. **Each car** when carrying its full complement of passengers weighed about **half a ton** which meant that the rope was 28 times above the actual working pressure.

Down the line, 106 road pulleys were fixed to ease the rope. It was also arranged that the rope was always one and three quarter times round the drum, equal to 30 feet of rope continually on the drum, so as to **prevent** any **possibility of a slip**. There was a six foot drum at the bottom of the line for the rope to go round which was endless being 800 yards long.

Courtesy of Shipley Glen Tramway.

Manufacturers and Suppliers

The rails were supplied by Messrs Perkins, Son and Barrett of Bradford; timber by Messrs Harrison and Singleton of Bradford; and the corrugated zinc which covered the engine house and car shed was supplied by Mr C. Bird of Luton.

The four passenger cars and a luggage car, were made by Sam Halliday and Sons of Baildon, the wheels having come from a well known foundry at Sheffield. These were fixed by means of pressure, keys being thus unnecessary, and the consequent risk of these working loose were avoided.

It had been expected that the cost of making and fitting the tramway would be about £500, but as a result of the necessary safety alterations and also of bad weather slowing down the progress of work, the cost was estimated to be closer to be beyond £1,000.

Sam Wilsons Own Words

In an interview with the Telegraph and Argus carried out on his 80th birthday, Sam told for the first time why he had built the railway:

"I had always been interested in the idea of running a little railway," he said," and I travelled all over the country to examine those which had been successfully established. It was on the little railway at Aberystwyth that my plans were based."

Here, he is referring to the Aberystwyth Cliff Railway which was built around the same time and opened in August 1896 as a funicular railway.

"Originally I had intended to build my own railway to the top of the moors in line with Victoria Road, Saltaire, but I found that I could not get consent from all the intervening land owners so I turned my attention to the path through Walker Woods to Shipley Glen:

The late Colonel Maude, Lord of Baildon Manor, then owner of Walker Woods, allowed me to build the tramway there and when I raised the question of rent he said, "What do you say to giving me £10 a year?" Needless to say; I jumped at the chance.

"I approached the late Sir James Roberts with the object of arranging for a supply of gas from the pipes which supplied Saltaire Mills. He agreed but seemed rather doubtful about the result of the experiment and said, "Whatever do you want to put a tramway up there for?" he asked. I told him there were seven reasons:

I am building it, I said, "for the old and the young, for the lame and the lazy, for the weak and the strong, and lastly for myself.

"We cleared the track by cutting down about 30 trees and removing a large number of rocks. Then we laid 600 yards of gas pipe from the Coach road. We had a difficult task. It was during a terrible winter when the ice was 18" thick.

Sam Halliday, of Baildon, built the original four cars, and the gas engine to haul the cars came from Shipley. Despite the fact that I did most of the work myself it cost about £2,500 to build, and most people seemed to think it would be a failure.

We opened out in 1895 and the tramway was a big success from the start. People who had not been strong enough, or energetic enough, to climb the hill through the woods began to visit the Glen regularly, and it became one of the most popular resorts for miles around.

Later on I built four new cars myself – and installed steel rails at £21 per yard to replace the original wooden track faced with, metal strips. The popularity of the Glen grew beyond all imagination. I remember one record Easter when I carried 114,500 passengers in five days. I had 14 men on my staff, working from 6am to midnight, and we were kept so busy that we had no time for meals.

When I retired in April, 1919, I had carried over 7,500,000 passengers without a single accident. I am very proud of this record, and I attribute it to the fact that I always observed 'safety first' principles, especially in the changing of cables."

Postscript

A significant local event took place in August 1904 when Emily Cooper (of **Coopers Tea Gardens** on Prod Lane) married Herbert Briggs a Science Master. Emily was the first bride to ride down the **tramway** to a horse drawn carriage waiting at the bottom to take her to her wedding at Baildon St John the Evangelist Church.

The **tramway** became a **hugely popular attraction** to visitors. In the 23 year period until Sam Wilson eventually sold it in 1919 it was estimated that it carried over 7,500,000 passengers.

Sam Wilson attempted to sell the tramway twice before eventually selling it in 1919. The first occasion was in **1910** when the advertisement stated *"Being sold as a going concern owing to owner wishing to retire."*

The second occasion was in August **1917** when the sale of the Tramway was withdrawn as the bidding reached £1,300. The advertisement stated that the nett estimated income per year was between £400 and £500. The auctioneers published details estimating that the average yearly income over a twenty year period was £700. In 1917 the yearly rent charged by the Lord of the Manor was £35 and the rates were £20. The lease was not due to expire until December 1925.

In 1919, stating his reason for **retiring** as **ill health,** Sam sold the business to Eddie and Mary Woodhead. Further details of the ownership of the Tramway are shown on page 106.

The Toboggan Slide - 1897

The second new ride was the Toboggan Slide. The Shipley Times and Express of 20th February, 1897 announced that:

"A plan of a proposed toboggan slide at the Glen for Mr S Wilson was referred to council."

No doubt inspired by the Toboggan Slide at the Saltaire Exhibition, Sam Wilson proposed to build on a grand scale: ***The Longest, Wildest and Steepest Toboggan Ride Ever Erected on Earth***. It was estimated that over one thousand tons of wood were used to construct the run.

This consisted of three wooden tracks which descended at an estimated **gradient of one in four** from the rocky escarpment at the top of the Glen to the valley floor at the bottom. Riders seated on **small wooden toboggans** would **hurtle down** the slide which ended in a slight uphill gradient intended to slow each toboggan down.

The riders then returned to the top of the Glen by a cable tram car, which also transported the empty toboggan in front, both being hauled back up the slope by a steel rope driven by a gas engine. The engine was manufactured and supplied by Cundall and Sons of Shipley.

Hideous?

A concerned reader registered unhappiness in the Bradford Daily Telegraph of 27th April, 1897 at the construction of the new ride:

*"The toboggan slide at Shipley Glen is a perfectly **hideous** blot on the landscape and is a **crude wooden structure** in the very **best part of the Glen.***

*It is time a **public authority** possessed the Glen and controlled the erection of aerial flights, slides, switchbacks etc. They might at least keep things on the fairground and not destroy the rusticity of the Glen proper."*

Unsightly Shanties?

Similar sentiments about all the rides, and specifically the toboggan, were expressed in an article in the Shipley Times and Express published ten days earlier:

*"Shipley Glen has now all the **appearance of a fair**. All who **appreciate** the **natural beauty** of the district will however have noticed that it is yearly having to bit by bit **concede** its **loveliness and freedom** to the vagaries of so-called amusement caterers.*

*It is not the merry-go-round or the cocoa-nut stall elements that come and go with the Easter festival which are the most objectionable. It is the erection of switchbacks, aerial flights and other unsightly shanties planked down as **"permanent works"** in some of the **prettiest parts** of the Glen and bidding fair before long to give the place the appearance of a **timber yard**.*

*The latest and worst offender in this line is the new **toboggan** slide, which cuts its way down among the rocks and trees, **marring** of course, as long as it stands, the **beauty** of the **whole surroundings**."*

Advice on the Building Plans

Sam Wilson consulted and took plans for the toboggan slide, to John Waugh, the Chartered Engineer who had carried out the safety tests on the Glen Tramway. On inspecting the plans, Waugh had commented: *You are making it strong enough; but you will have all sorts of apes, idiots and fools to contend with."*

This was to be proved true in August 1899, when one of the riders on the toboggan, a Bradford waiter who had been sitting on the knee of a friend despite being warned not to do so, damaged his suit when the toboggan he was riding on stopped suddenly. He took the matter to court and received a token award.

However, such complaints were essentially insignificant compared to what happened next!

A Serious Accident

On Whit Monday 1900, one of the cable tram cars returning passengers up the steep incline to the top of the Glen, accidentally caught and ran over the cable, causing it to snap.

The car which was carrying twelve people ran back down the slope at speed and crashed through the wooden barrier at the bottom. Seven people were seriously injured and admitted to Sir Titus Salt's Hospital, Saltaire with broken bones, severe lacerations and bruises.

As a result, the ride was closed and eventually dismantled within a year as was the Aerial Flight, essentially at the request of Bradford Corporation who from 1900 would be the new owners of large tracts of Baildon Common and Shipley Glen.

Local Politics?

All the previous points made by various commentators regarding **defacement** of the Glen, and **safety** of the rides were brought into **context** by the following comment in the Shipley Times and Express, three days after the accident:

"Shipley Glen has enjoyed such a remarkable immunity from serious accidents, in spite of the tremendous crowds of visitors to be seen there at every public holiday attended by fine weather...

The toboggan accident on Tuesday night created a more painful sensation than would otherwise have been the case. The public have become gradually accustomed to sensational contrivances for their amusement, first by the aerial flight, which was followed by the cable tramway and afterwards by the toboggan itself.

The only accident hitherto recorded in connection with the use of this "longest, widest and steepest toboggan ride ever erected on earth" as the proprietor proudly described it, had the result of wrecking a suit, for which the owner sought and received compensation.

The accident on Tuesday raises one or two interesting questions. Great objections were raised when the tramway and toboggan were allowed to be erected to the utter defacement of two of the most charming bits of that portion of Baildon known as "Shipley Glen." The then Lord of the Manor however, gave permission for the erection of these structures in the teeth of adverse public sentiment... the point on which many people would like to be enlightened is how far the new owners of the manorial rights, Bradford Corporation, may be willing to permit the defacement of the landscape to be continued?

If the structures cannot be compulsorily removed, it would be interesting to know if there is any means of enforcing a strict and frequent inspection of such things by independent persons, in the interests of public safety.

Toboggan Slide after the accident.

2 - INTERESTS OF THE DIFFERENT PARTIES USING THE GLEN

As detailed elsewhere, local politics was just one of the drivers of the changes which would occur next. Before examining the effects of change of ownership effected by Bradford Corporation, it would be useful to set the scene by summarising the interests of the different constituents potentially using the Glen, and the dilemmas arising.

Lord of the Manor

By 1900 the Lord of the Manor, Colonel Maude had been involved in charging rents to showmen and speculators for stalls on the plateau and for the Aerial Flight, Glen Tramway and the Toboggan for some years. He had also been in negotiation with Bradford Corporation in conjunction with Baildon and Shipley, to sell specific Manorial Rights to Baildon Common and Shipley Glen. This he managed successfully in April 1900 whilst still managing to retain specified land interests in the locality.

Speculators

The speculators on each of the major rides and attractions had in essence spotted money making ventures/new ideas. These were intended to provide novel attractions and experiences which would attract growing numbers of workers from throughout West Yorkshire to the Glen. There was obviously always an element of risk in doing so, but the energy of the speculators in bringing their ideas to fruition brought new opportunities to the area.

Show-people

With the demise of many town based Fairs in the mid 1800s, showpeople sought new venues such as common land on which to run a variety of stalls, competitions, sports, catering and games of chance. The advent of the steam engine also helped to produce motive power for roundabouts and other such attractions. Easter and Whitsun Bank Holidays became a profitable time when good venues could attract tens of thousands of eager holidaymakers intent on enjoying themselves.

Local Residents

Some local residents particularly those living close to the Glen and Baildon Common saw the obvious potential of catering for those visiting the Glen or walking over the moors. Hence the early proliferation of Temperance Hotels and tearooms. Later this would extend to public house and farmhouse catering on some of the popular walking routes. After 1900 smaller and more passive attractions such as Vulcan House Pleasure Grounds and the Japanese Gardens would be successfully introduced and run by local residents.

It should also be remembered that local residents were also rate-payers and many of those who complained about the invasion by thousands of visitors to the area, had every right to do so.

Not only was the previously peaceful and beautiful countryside in which they lived, drastically altered by the erection of new and very visible new rides and attractions, but the noise and disruption of the fairground brought its own problems. Toilet facilities and running water were always an issue as the Glen was not a "managed" pleasure ground area and as such had no adequate provision for many thousands of visitors. Litter left by the visitors and show-people was also a problem with only the goodwill of local people in tidying up as a solution.

The Yorkshire Evening Post of 6th June 1899 summed up the dilemma:

"There were insanitary conditions on the common at the Glen, which after Easter was aptly described as the Baildon midden. For the last fourteen days a large number of show people camped out at the Glen, for whom there was no accommodation...these, with recent encroachments on the common, threaten to convert a pretty spot into a nuisance for those residing locally."

The Visitors

Through visitors spending their hard earned wages in the area, there were obvious financial benefits for the local economy.

Initially the attractions of the countryside/nature in terms of the Glen being regarded as a local "lung" for thousands of industrial process workers, offering subsequent health benefits, seemed sufficient.

However, technological advances and the vogue for a variety of new and thrilling experiences changed public expectations - hence the introduction of new rides. To have these and a large fairground in the same place as well was just too good an opportunity to miss!

Several newspaper articles captured the flavour:

*"Popularising the Glen and **new attractions** such as the toboggan... **They are clearly wanted or they would not be there**... nature has to be supplemented by other attractions. It is a symptom of the age."*

The next noted:- *"There was a strong smell of oil coming from the direction of the toboggan slide, but the **large numbers** of people seemed not to notice... the **switchback, aerial flight, toboggan** and **fairground** were **objects of much more attention** than the beautiful scenery and **nature took a back seat."***

Another observed:- *Should the **Glen be freed** of its various **sensational monstrosities? Deprived of these what would Shipley Glen be to a Bank Holiday crowd?***

Romance?

Besides family, works, Church and Sunday School outings, the Glen was also a major attraction for men and women seeking opportunities of a more "romantic nature" It was renowned as a place where young people could "court" away from the strictures of parental control. For many the Glen also offered an opportunity to escape the confines of a tedious job, the unhealthy city and cramped housing and to enjoy individual freedom and adventure.

It is not the intention of this book to expand on this area of the history of the Glen. However around 1900 a local composer Jimmy Sutton and a music hall comedian, singer and lyricist, Reg Bolton wrote:

Meet me Gwen upon Shipley Glen

He was a shy young Yorkshire lad,
And he lived on **Baildon Moor**.
She wore a 'pill' from Lister's Mill
They met and his heart grew sore.
She shyly said her name was Gwen,
And she didn't mind meeting him again.
He plucked up courage to write a note
And this is what the young swain wrote.

Meet me Gwen on **Shipley Glen**
On Sunday afternoon
Near 'number nine' we'll have a good time, **
And return by the light of the moon.
You'll enjoy it up there
'Cos you'll get the **salt aire**
And you'll fancy you're out by the sea
Then if you're willing and I have a shilling
We'll call at **Dick Hudson's** for tea.
They sat next Sunday on the Glen.
Said the maid with drooping head,
I've never been up here before.
Then with shame all the ferns turned red
As he told the tale to the saucy minx
The rocks exchanged such knowing winks,
When he slipped on her finger a 'gold brass ring'
The little birds began to sing
Meet me Gwen…

** number-nine is a large gritstone boulder which was reputedly *"a place where foolish couples met."*

Perhaps this sentiment as a metaphor signalled the beginning of a gentler start to a new Century.

3 - EDWARDIAN ERA NEW CENTURY - NEW OWENERSHIP - 1900

This section outlines the transfer of the Manorial Rights to Bradford Council and the initial impact, which served to later change the nature of what was offered to visitors to the Glen.

The 1876 Commons Act

This Act essentially set out an initial framework for a change of ownership affecting both Shipley Glen and Baildon Moor.

Enlightenment as regards **common land** came in the second half of the 1800s as a result of **towns** growing and **spreading their boundaries** further and further out. As a **safeguard** to that land the **1876 Commons Act** was introduced. This resulted legally in increasing care being taken to ensure that private interests were not allowed to rob the people of common land and open spaces by enclosing them, whatever the justification of owners of the soil.

By sheer coincidence, 1876 was also the year that Colonel Maude had inherited the title Lord of the Manor on the death of his father.

The Bradford Tramways and Improvement Act 1899

After protracted and **complicated negotiations** between the Lord of the Manor, Bradford Corporation and Baildon and Shipley Local Boards (under the auspices of The Bradford Tramways and Improvement Act 1899), **Baildon Moor and Shipley Glen** were **purchased by Bradford Corporation**. The purchase price was seven thousand pounds.

Colonel Maude finally agreed to sell 770 acres of common land in Baildon, which included Baildon Moor, parts of Baildon Green and Brackenhall. Initially, 50 acres were to be reconveyenced to the Lord of the Manor and 50 were to be disposed of by the Bradford Corporation to raise funds.

The land would be:

*"Held by Bradford Corporation, and at all times **kept open, unenclosed and unbuilt on** and subject to the exercise of all pasture gates and existing common rights thereon the open spaces for the recreation and enjoyment of the public."*

That statement only summarises the main aspects of the Improvement Act as there were numerous clauses specifying what could and could not be done on the land and by whom and over what timescales. The Act eventually went before Parliament. The moor was to be managed by a joint board consisting of six Bradford Corporation and two Baildon and two Shipley councillors.

Transport

In 1898 the Bradford Corporation introduced the **first electric trams** to the city and horse drawn and steam trams were phased out by 1903. Trolley buses (1911) and motorbuses would eventually replace earlier forms of transport.

Building of a Road

Bradford Corporation agreed to build a road from Glen Gate over Bracken Hall Green to join the Bingley Road at/near Lobley Gate and from the Glen towards Eldwick Beck at Loadpit Gate. If they failed to complete the road in two years, the Lord of the Manor would receive a further £1,000. If it was completed the Lord of the Manor would contribute £500.

Toboggan Slide

The agreement also allowed Sam Wilson (who was according to Colonel Maude's 1898 records paying £10 a year rent), the rights to operate the toboggan slide for a further three years. In the event this did not happen because of the toboggan accident.

For Sale

On 29th August, 1900, two months after the accident, the Yorkshire

Post and Leeds Intelligencer carried the following advertisement:

"To be sold by Tender, the Whole of the TOBOGGAN SLIDE at Shipley Glen together with Petroleum Engine, Cars etc; the whole to be removed within three calendar months from the date of acceptance of the Tender.

Notice to Quit

A couple of weeks later an article appeared in the Bradford Times of 8th September 1900 stating:

*"Now that **Bradford Corporation** have come into possession of Shipley Glen they intend to clear away any unsightly erections and to preserve so far as possible natural beauty. They have decided to give **notice to quit** to the owners of the **Aerial Flight** and **Toboggan Slide** and to request removal of these structures at the earliest possible date."*

Auction

Advertisements in the Yorkshire Post and Leeds Intelligencer on 17th and 24th November, 1900 announced the following sale items:

"Shipley Glen Near Bradford
The whole of the WOODWORK which formed the structure of the Toboggan and Aerial Flight in lots
Comprising of 100 tons of pitch pine, redwood and deal scantling. 2000 square yards of floor boards, 2000 yards of wire rope, half a ton of lead piping. Also a 12 horse-power oil engine by Cundall and Sons Ltd, Shipley."

Some of the other advertisements placed at the time stated wrongly that it was wood from the Ocean Wave Switchback for sale. The continuing existence of the Switchback is confirmed by an advertisement in the Bradford Daily Telegraph on 26th February, 1901 asking for estimates to be submitted for painting it.

Correspondence

Correspondence in the newspapers over the period late 1900 until 1902 was generally complementary to Bradford Corporation and the Joint Board as regards getting rid of the "**unsightly**" rides. Positive comment was also made about attempts to return the area to its former natural beauty.

Despite attempts by the Corporation to maintain the natural beauty of Glen and its surrounds there were still two bones of contention:

1. The Fair

A typical example of comment was made in the Shipley Times and Express of 25th April, 1902:

"Nothing will tend to restore the glory of this delightful spot so much as putting a stop – prohibiting altogether – the carnival held at Eastertide.

It is a growth of comparatively recent years, and the place has deteriorated every year since it began. Not only has the showman changed very largely the character of the crowds who used to visit the Glen at that period of the year, but he leaves behind sad reminders of his occupancy."

The article then describes the types of rubbish left and suggests that a couple of men with wheelbarrows should be employed to clear up the mess.

2. The New Road

A petition to Baildon Council was made in 1902 regarding the state of the roads approaching the Glen. In April of that year a contract was advertised by Bradford Corporation for building a stone bridge over Lodepit Beck.

Throughout 1903 and 1904 the newspapers carried reports on the cost and building of road provision and the negotiations as regards who contributed what towards these. The work was started on 19th October, 1904 and amongst the workforce were fifty unemployed men from Bradford.

The Eventual Demise of the Fair

The road proved to be an instant success and led to ten years of much improved access to the Glen.

However, significant damage to the road by showmen's vehicles transporting heavy machinery and rides to the plateau would lead in 1914 to Bradford Corporation banning such traffic from using the road. This in turn would lead to the demise of the Fair on the scale that it had been previously been held, and is covered on page 95.

Vulcan House - 1905

Early Tea room

Vulcan House was built by the **Perry** family in 1879 and run as a modest tearoom in the garden. Records suggest that basic amusements and hand powered roundabouts were added about 1882. Known as Perry's Vulcan House, Jane Perry the first wife of John William Perry (until her death in 1888) and then his second wife, **Elizabeth** Perry (married 1890), gradually built the business up establishing it as a flourishing **tearoom**, particularly at **Bank Holidays**. By 1901 Vulcan House was also being used as a starting point for many local harriers races.

Development

In **1905** Elizabeth started **advertising** on a larger scale, initially trying to attract Sunday School and Other Parties *"who will find every convenience at Mrs Perry's Vulcan House - Shipley Glen."*

Bioscope Cinema

In the same year, Benjamin Roberts, Elizabeth's son by her first marriage started up the **Vulcan Bioscope Company** run from Vulcan House. Besides eventually organising exhibitions in a large tent in the garden he also demonstrated film equipment locally. In August of **1905** he also advertised nationally, wanting to buy 10,000 feet of second-hand film for his new enterprise. In December of that year he organised a **film show** for the **Salts Pensioners Charity**. He carried on this side of the business until he put Vulcan House up for sale in 1913.

Rides

On 20th April 1906 The Wharfedale and Airedale Observer reported that Vulcan House had the following rides:

Cape to Cairo Railway (which was the Aerial Glide by another name), a **Bicycle Roundabout, Donkeys** and a **Water Wheel**.

Sunday Trading

Elizabeth Perry was not afraid of **challenging authority** as regards her business. On three occasions in April and May of **1906** she was prosecuted under the **Lords Day Observance Act**, for Sunday trading. On each occasion she was fined 2/6d.

On the first occasion in answer to the charge she said that she would be willing to close any day other than Sunday and that it would be profitable for her to pay a **small fine continually** as a sort of **Sunday trading rent**.

On the second occasion she told Magistrates that it was **absolutely necessary** for her to keep open on **Sundays** as **people required refreshments**. She asked if she could serve **people who had travelled three miles**, but the Bench declined to express an opinion.

On the third occasion police reported that they had found her serving seven people with sweets and cigarettes from a shop attached to her house, where she ran a regular business.

On **researching this further** I discovered an article in the Wharfedale and Airedale Observer of 10th **August 1906** which suggests that Elizabeth was presenting herself as a **test case** as regards interpretation of legislation. I also think that she knew about possible changes when she took the action that she did. The article stated:

"Small shopkeepers...who have conducted business in the neighbourhood of Shipley Glen will be deeply interested in the report of the Joint Committee of the House of Lords and Commons on the question of Sunday trading...at present there is little evidence to show that such trading causes inconvenience to its opponents...the Committee find that Sunday trading has increased."

Whilst the Committee recommended that **Sunday trading be kept** they also suggested that **exceptions** should be made in any future Parliamentary Bill. Summarised, these were:

- Recognition of the fact that *"many of the traders who have opened their premises on a Sunday have taken respite from their business on some other day."*

- To permit sale of refreshments - sweets, newspapers, medicines, milk, cream, ice, vegetables, bread, fruit, fish, during part of the day, subject to local byelaws.

- As regards tobacco and pipes, sale should only be allowed during hours in which public houses were licensed to be open.

Each of these points were in effect those raised by Elizabeth when she appeared in Court on the three occasions. She obviously had an excellent business sense and knowledge of what was going on.

Ambulance Station

As regards public service Mrs Perry was also astute enough to also offer her premises for other uses. At Easter 1907 she *"kindly placed a wooden shop at the disposal of the Shipley and District Corps of the St John Ambulance Association"* who were on duty and patrolling the Glen plateau. They stored their equipment in the shop and used it as their headquarters and treatment room for four days. A sheet placed on the ground outside the shop was used to collect donations for their services.

Courtesy of Shipley Glen Tramway.

Vulcan House Pleasure Grounds For Sale

Elizabeth Perry died in January 1912 at the age of 75 having run Vulcan House Tearoom and Pleasure Gardens for eighteen years. Her will named her son Benjamin and John Cox (a photographer) as her beneficiaries.

In May 1913 Benjamin put the business up for sale, profiling the unique and beautiful position and the length of time that the business had been run successfully. He also highlighted that the property had its own electric light and gas plants and a private water supply.

Besides the house, the following was offered:

"A Sweet Shop, Refreshment Room, Photographers Shop, Large Tent used for Cinematograph, Swings, Roundabout and a contrivance known as "The Cape to Cairo Railway."

In June 1913 at the auction of Vulcan House Pleasure Grounds and Refreshment Rooms, the property was withdrawn from sale at a price of £1,400. Benjamin was shown on the West Yorkshire Electoral Rolls for 1914 and 1915 as living at Vulcan House. Small items from the Pleasure Grounds were advertised for sale in 1916 and 1917.

1918 - 2005 Postscript

West Yorkshire Electoral Rolls also show that John Cox the photographer named in Elizabeth's will, continued to live in Vulcan House as his abode and to run his photographers shop from **1918** until 1927. It is likely that he actually lived and worked there from 1913 onwards but some records of addresses and businesses were for reasons of security, not made available for the war period 1914 to 1917. Vulcan House was also split up into apartments where two families lived from 1918 until **1937**.

George and Jane Voss are shown in Electoral Records as living at Vulcan House from 1918 until 1937 and were running the Pleasure Ground side of the business during this period. George and Jane according to the 1911 Census were Publicans in Bradford. Jane died in 1936. George is shown in 1939 pre World War Two records as a Retired Caterer now living in Harrogate. He died there in 1941.

In **1942** the Vulcan House Pleasure Grounds were again put up for sale advertising the following:

"A Retail Shop, brick built Tearoom, small lean-to Tearoom, two ranges of Swings, Aerial Glide and a large Aviary."

Again war records preclude any mention in the West Yorkshire Electoral Rolls of names and addresses of businesses. However, from 1945 Harry Teale is recorded as living and working at the Pleasure Grounds which he expanded to include new roundabouts, rides and slot machines. He also added a small zoo/menagerie which contained two lions, introduced in the late 1940s, early 1950's and up until 1955 also included Billy, a Himalayan Mountain Bear.

Courtesy of Mike Lawson.

In 1967 he sold the business to his nephew Paul Teale who continued the enterprise until he leased the Pleasure Grounds to the Breeze family in 1985, who then ran them until they were closed in 2005.

Japanese Gardens - 1905

Early Development - A Tranquil Setting

One of the much loved amusements at the Glen did not owe its origins to the need for thrills or excitement as some of the other early rides did. Instead it offered a more tranquil and sedate pace of passage in quiet and landscaped surroundings. This experience was known as the Japanese Gardens and was the brainchild of Thomas (Tom) Hartley of Bowling, Bradford.

Prior to being proprietor of the Japanese Gardens, he is identified in the 1871 Census as a General Dealer living and working in Bowling in Bradford and in 1881 as an Ironmonger still living in Bowling.

Ivy House – Prod Lane

In 1886 Tom went to live at Ivy House, Prod Lane, Baildon with his wife Hannah and family. According to rumour and local knowledge, Hartley was a businessman friend of Titus Salt's son, Titus Junior. When Hartley's wife became ill, Salt seemingly advised him to move to Shipley Glen for the quality of the air.

At the time, Japanese Gardens were very fashionable and were being built in the grounds of large houses around the country. Possibly stimulated by the Japanese Village at the Saltaire Exhibition and partly to provide interest for his invalid wife, Tom built his own version of a Japanese Garden in the grounds of Ivy House.

In the 1891 Census he is described as a Wood Dealer and in 1901 as a Market Gardener, both of which would bring in income. It was not until 1905 that he advertised the Japanese Gardens as such.

Not Japanese but...

A feature in the Shipley Times and Express of 20th May 1904 stated:

"The Illustrated Mail says: The Japanese are the only people in the world who make a speciality of miniature landscape construction in small gardens. The Japanese Plan has been closely followed in at least one British garden – that of Ivy House – Shipley Glen, Yorkshire.

There, a pretty bit of scenery has been compressed into a very small space, a miniature castle standing on a miniature island in a miniature lake. Every part of this "scenery" has been constructed by the owner, Mr. T. Hartley.

Advertising

In May, June and July 1905 his advertisement described:

Hartleys Japanese Gardens - Shipley Glen
The most novel and interesting gardens in the district
Photographic Studio - Sailing Boats for Children - Swings - Grotto etc

The Castle and Arches

Tom built a pond with islands in the middle, on which he constructed a small folly in the shape of a ruined castle and surrounded by rustic arches. The castle and 8 arches were built from clinker, the cinders forming one of the first concrete structures built in the area. These structures were covered with white lime. In an attempt to give them a rough and rustic appearance he used the waste dross reputedly taken from the fireboxes of the steam trains which travelled from Bradford to Saltaire. Locals observed him wheeling the material by the barrow-load through the woods and up the hill.

The castle was large enough for 6/7 people to enter at the same time and had a chime of bells operated by a penny in the slot mechanism.

The Lake/Pond

The Pond was set in the midst of beautifully landscaped flower beds. For a small charge a boatman would stand upright and propel passengers in a flat bottomed boat big enough to take 12 to 15 children, (originally called the Saucy Sue) around a number of circuits. Two circuits of the pond were 1d.

Near the pond and still in line with his wife's bedroom window Hartley built a smaller pond with a large fountain, surrounded by archways over the paths and below the second pond was a water-lily pool, a watercress pool and rose-beds.

The water for the ponds was provided by a stream running down Hope Hill from the top of Baildon Moor, which he diverted and rechanneled so that the water was flowing continuously.

Further back from the ponds were four glass houses, one with a stream running through and a small waterfall with an enormous hydrangea and other plants. The others housed an aviary containing a talking parrot, exotic birds, love birds and doves. There was also a grotto which housed a polyphon playing tunes or bells and a phonograph worked with a water wheel. Between them was a small amusement arcade with penny slot machines, cases of old curiosities, Indian butterflies on a mounted display and other exhibits.

Tom Hartley working on the early development of the Japanese Gardens.

Hartley filled the garden near the photographers studio with trees including lilac, orange blossom and laburnum complimented by a rose garden and 300 to 400 roses and many other beautiful flowers. At the back of Ivy House he built a tea room which had a hut, with long wooden tables and wooden benches as seats plus swings and seesaws. In a cellar workshop Tom Hartley made bird tables with thatched roofs, rustic furniture and dove-cotes, all of which were for sale.

Advertising and Postcards

Tom obviously had an eye for marketing the various aspects of his gardens as the advertisement opposite from 1904 shows.

In it you can see him working in the garden below the window from which his wife would have viewed the garden pond. Also advertised are swings (these were boat swings), see-saws and the grotto. The enterprise also offered the opportunity for visitors to have their photograph professionally taken on a plate camera using the gardens as a backdrop. Failing this, Tom also sold postcards of the gardens and pond.

Cut flowers and bouquets from the garden were also sold to visitors.

In March 1905 at the age of 60 he remarried and his wedding certificate identifies him then as a Photographer marrying Elsie Rushworth aged 41 at Otley Road Wesleyan Methodist Chapel.

. . HARTLEYS' . .

JAPANESE GARDENS,

SHIPLEY GLEN.

Visitors to the Glen should on no account fail to visit these **Novel** and **Interesting Gardens**. Ample provision for their amusement and enjoyment is provided, consisting of

SWINGS, SEE-SAWS, GROTTO, Etc.

Picturesque Photographic Studio with Rustic Background.

Where you may have a Photograph taken which will do both justice to yourself and to the photographer.

Miniature Circular Lake
On which is a small boat that has proved a great favourite with both young and old.

Cut Flowers & Bouquets.

Do not fail to make a call and we venture to say that you will not regret it.

Closed entirely on Sundays.

The advert also shows that the gardens were "closed entirely on Sundays." This was because the Hartleys were staunch Methodists. In later years under other owners the gardens would be open on Sundays.

Changes In Ownership

After his first wife Hannah died and when Tom remarried he built a one storey bungalow called Edenberry for himself and his new wife and a bungalow for his son at the back of the gardens.

In 1913 Madam de Laurie a Horoscope reader and Palmist advertised that she was carrying out interviews at the Japanese Gardens and in October 1913 J. T .Clark advertised apartments to let at the Japanese Tea Gardens, Shipley Glen.

The Japanese Gardens as an entity were **sold by Tom Hartley** on his retirement to Tom Clark who initially advertised them as Shipley Glen Wonderland. At this time they contained a refreshment cafe, swings, a grotto, boating and other amusements.

Courtesy of Bingley and District Local History Society.

In 1915 two children's events were held on the Glen, the first for the Shipley Soldiers and Sailors Wives Club. In June, 100 wives and children of serving men played rounders and went on the swings and see-saws at Tom Clarks Japanese Tea Gardens, then enjoyed a substantial tea. The photograph below captures the event.

In September a Poor Law Childrens Party was held on the Glen. The children and their carers were taken up the **Glen Tramway** to the **Japanese Gardens** where they played on the swings and see-saws and then played football and cricket on the **Glen plateau.**

Tom Clark lived at Ivy House until 1918 when he decided to divide the gardens into two. In one part he built a bungalow for himself, which was in line with the two that Tom Hartley had built. He retained the boat and swings for himself and opened a baker's and confectioner's shop at the side of the bungalow.

He sold Ivy House, the other half of the garden and the tea rooms to Harry Clark who then ran the tearooms until 1924. From that date ownership then passed to the Theakston brothers, first John and on his early death, George.

Postscript
A Bingley Childs Memories of the Japanese Gardens

The late Winnie Harrison (author of *Day's Awake - Childhood Memories of Bingley* (1997) recalled visits to the gardens in the 1920's:

"Our first objective was the lake. Tea could wait, so could the swings and see-saws just inside the gate... The lake was very small, no more than twelve feet wide and thirty feet long, with an island looking as Japanese as it could look in the uplands of the West Riding of Yorkshire. For a penny or two pence, according to size, a middle aged boatman punted children twice round the island. Great trepidation seized the more timorous voyagers as they stepped in or out of this rocking craft."

1930's and 1940s

Fondly remembered family memories of this period include annual visits to the gardens and pond by the Blind Institute in Bradford and of many Sunday Schools. The venue was also frequented by cycling clubs from throughout Yorkshire who would arrive and spend their day in the gardens and on the moors, having pots of tea at the start and end of their day.

Victory in Europe Day in 1945 was celebrated by many locals who visited Shipley Glen resulting in queues of upwards of five hundred visitors at the Japanese Garden Tearooms at one time.

Japanese Gardens, 1954.

Beginning of the End

It appears that after the Second World War it became harder to make a go of the enterprise although throughout the 1950s The Glen was still a popular destination. The photograph on the previous page taken in 1954 shows that boating was still a feature of a visit to the Japanese Gardens.

Over time the once glorious gardens began to deteriorate as the advent of the car meant that fewer visitors came to the area. The original house and gardens were sold in 1975 and the land used for housing development.

Tom Hartley the original and proud creator of the Japanese Gardens died at the age of 94 in 1937. He like the many visitors over the years would have been saddened by the eventual demise of this much loved local attraction, despite the attempts of the final owners to maintain the gardens as a popular attraction.

Perhaps the final words are best left with the Grandaughter of the Theakston brothers, Margaret Ellis and her family memories of the Japanese Gardens:

"Now all that is left of the late Victorian/early Edwardian pleasure gardens are older folks' memories of halcyon summer days when they were young and their recollections of the warmth and happiness of a lost age."

The Farms 1904 - 1906

Around the same time as Vulcan House and the Japanese Gardens were advertising and new road and path approaches to the Glen were also being developed, many of the local farms also saw opportunities for trade.

Some of these had like Vulcan House previously provided refreshments in a modest fashion to visitors. Some decided to try their luck at new ventures.

Whilst there were other farms/houses providing teas and catering in the Glen area, this section identifies those farms which were advertising in the Victorian/Edwardian period when visitor numbers were at their height.

Lucy Hall Farm

This farm was owned by the Lord of the Manor and had previously been farmed by Jacob Denby. In 1901 the farm was let and tenanted by Henry Ackroyd and his wife Ellen. Included in the letting information was a statement that "*Shipley Glen visitors are good customers for dairy produce.*"

During 1905 the farm frequently advertised: *Lucy Hall Farm - Teas Provided, Small Parties Catered For - Splendid Situation. H. Ackroyd, Shipley Glen.*

No further advertising followed.

Golcar Farm

James Steel and his wife Lily moved to Golcar Farm around 1898. By 1900 they were advertising *New Special accommodation for visitors.* From 1902 to 1906 they developed *Apartments in a Farmhouse Near to the Glen and the Moors*, and by 1906 their advertisements had added *Golf Links and Bath* to the statement. In the same year they advertised for an Assistant to help with the business.

By 1914 they had further added *Refreshment Rooms and Afternoon Teas* as well as *Board and Residence* and were still advertising as such in 1927. James put the business including the farm, stock and catering equipment up for sale in 1935. Both he and Lily died in 1946.

Golcar Farm.

Crook Farm

John Bentley Lancaster and his wife Emma started providing teas to walkers on a small scale in 1888 and by 1901 were advertising *Parties catered for and Teas Provided*. By **1905** they had employed an assistant for the tearoom. Unfortunately John died in 1906 and and Emma in 1910. John Ellis Lancaster and his wife Harriett ran **picnics and teas** at the Farm in the period from 1906 onwards. The business was put up for sale in 1911 and then withdrawn and was then again put up for sale in **1913** as the *Sale of a Well Known Refreshment House which is a considerable business providing refreshments*. Catering was still being provided until 1916 in the form of picnics.

Crook Farm.

Crook Farm.

Postscript

The farm then had three different families living there in the period between 1917 and 1935. Members of the Lancaster family, namely Bill, David and Constance returned to live there from 1936.

From 1946 the farm developed **camping** facilities (initially for the Scouts) and a year later sought permission from Baildon Urban District Council to allow **weekend huts** and **summer bungalows** on the site. Records show that permission was again requested in 1947, 1948, 1949, 1952, 1954 and 1958. In 1956 an application was also made for the renewal of the licence for a camping site for three years.

Baildon Urban District Council granted planning permission for a caravan park in 1961.

Brackenhall Farm

This farm was **owned** by the **Lord of the Manor** and up until 1901 had been tenanted and farmed by the Walker family. It was not initially transferred to Bradford Corporation and remained for some years as part of the **estate of Colonel Maude**.

Walter Major Marsden, the new tenant, was an Honorary Bailiff and Steward of the Lord of the Manor and eventually became Bailiff of

Baildon Moor and Shipley Glen under Bradford Corporation. In **1902** he began offering afternoon **tea at weekends and Bank holidays** at Brackenhall Farm and also developed cricket and football competitions in the grounds of the farm.

Brackenhall Farm.

Perhaps his most ambitious venture was in **1906** when he organized a series of **Summer Concerts** which was the first time such entertainment had been offered on the Glen. These were advertised and run in May, June and July 1906 and were in effect **variety shows.** A large advertisement in the Shipley Times and Express in May featured:

Shipley Glen Open-Air Concerts - During Summer Months
In the Field near The Switchback
The First Concert will be given on Whit Saturday June 2nd 1906
A Refined Programme of Songs, Duets, Jokes and Concerted Pieces
Special Engagement - "The Three Periwinks."
Living Liliputians, Paper Manipulators and Burlesque Conjurors
On Whit Monday
The International Dancers - Joe and Nellie Rhodes - Skipping Rope Dancers
On Whit Sunday - Grand Sacred Concerts at 3pm and 7pm

The Sunday Concerts were organised after Sunday morning Church hours and were of a more "classical" nature. They featured the Brackenhall Orchestra or the Bradford Theatre Orchestra and several local opera singers. After evening performances on weekdays there was opportunity for dancing between 9pm and 10pm.

Mr Marsden also advertised "*If the weather is unpropitious the Concerts will be held in a Commodious Marquee specially secured for the occasion.*" He also stated that no expense had been spared, but also that there was a collection at the gate to defray expenses.

There is no record of him organising similar events after 1906.

Assault

At Easter 1907 another matter which caused **concern** within the local community raised its head. Unless visitors or showmen brought water with them to the Glen, there was **no running water supply**. Consequently it was only through the good nature of residents that water could be obtained.

The Leeds Mercury of 6th April, 1907 reported an incident:

"For some time past Mr Walter M Marsden, a special constable appointed by Bradford Corporation at Brackenhall Farm has supplied the showmen on Shipley Glen with water. Lately however he has been subjected to a good deal of annoyance and he decided to charge 1d a bucket. This was resented by some of the showmen."

The article then explains that one of them took objection to this and hit Mr Marsden on the jaw, knocking him out. The Magistrate in jailing the accused for two weeks hard labour, said that he did not know of any conceivable excuse for striking such violent blows on a private premises, when taking something that belonged to another person.

The next year, the Shipley Times and Express reported on 22nd May 1908 that the Baildon District Council Water Committee had approved the fitting of a water service pipe to the main at the top of Prod Lane. This was intended to supply water for stallholders at the Easter fair.

25 Years Service

Mr Marsden was regarded as one of the best known and interesting characters in the district, who for many years served tea on home built rustic tables in his garden. He was also a talented artist whose work was exhibited at Bradford Town Hall.

As Manor Bailiff for 25 years his duties were to patrol, superintend and safeguard Baildon Moor and Shipley Glen and the roads leading there. It was recognised that he knew both like the back of his hand, a fact which would serve him well when his eyesight began to fail him in later life when he still patrolled the area. He died at the farm in 1932.

Postscript

It appears that having previously been known as Brackenhall, the name has at some period made the transition and is now known as Bracken Hall.

Several families lived at the Farm or in its cottages between 1932 and 1946. Frank Thompson Ackroyd lived at Bracken Hall from 1947 until he died there in May 1977.

Bracken Hall Farm is now lived in by the Illingworth family and Bracken Hall House is run as a Luxury Bed and Breakfast establishment by Sally Illingworth. The Bracken Hall Countryside Centre is run at weekends at the side of the house. Further details of Bracken Hall House are shown on page 114 and further details of the Countryside Centre are shown on page 115.

The Fairs 1906 - 1921

When the Glen Fairs originally started, what was on offer was fairly simple entertainment, mainly consisting of shows rather than rides.

However as noted by The National Fair and Circus Archive, University of Sheffield (2018):

"By the end of the Victorian era the landscape of the fairground was populated by all kinds of rides, switchbacks and gallopers... Mechanisation shifted the emphasis from "shows", which were rooted in the past, to rides which gave

the showmen freedom to keep in step with the technological advances of an ever revolutionary age."

One thing that had not changed was the fact that in 1907 the Manor Bailiff Jeremiah Garnett was still advertising that showmen and others had to contact and pay him if they wanted spaces on the Glen for the Easter holidays.

To patrons, their perception of the **"Glen"** now offered the Glen Tramway, Vulcan House Pleasure Grounds, the Japanese Gardens and the Switchback in addition to the Fairground attractions. In 1906 and 1907 these included:

- Photographic Studios
- Motor Car roundabouts
- Gallopers (Horse inspired roundabouts) and hobby horses
- Velocipedes
- Switchbacks
- Temporary Aerial Flights
- Shooting Galleries
- Boxing Shows
- Goal kicking competitions
- Penny Gaffs
- Knock em Down's (coconut shies) and Aunt Sallies
- Swings and High Flyer Swing boats
- Palmists and Fortune Tellers
- Refreshment stalls
- Donkey and Horse Rides

The area now had access roads by which the showmen could transport their sometimes large and heavy rides. However there was no electricity or gas laid on to power rides or equipment and many of the larger roundabouts were therefore by necessity still steam powered. Smaller rides would have been hand powered.

100,000 Visitors!

On 5th April, 1907 both the Shipley Times and Express and the Airedale and Wharfedale Observer reported that a crowd estimated at over 100,000 had visited the Fair at the Glen on Easter Monday. The Observer noted:

"There were one or two new inventions of the "aerial flight." I caught sight of one well known Baildon lad seated on what seemed like a chair suspended from a wire trolley rope carried on poles, and being whirled round at a great pace. At the Glen there was indeed "all the fun of the fair." The high flyers, roundabouts and penny shows were doing good business."

A Missed Opportunity?

On 5th June, 1908 the Observer reported on a major political event held on the Glen:

"There have been many monster holiday crowds at Shipley Glen but in the opinion of most people all records were broken on Sunday last when an open-air demonstration was held at the popular resort by the National Women's Social and Political Union." Namely the Suffragettes.

The newspaper describes how the crowd that eventually gathered on the Glen plateau was variously estimated at between 50,000 and 75,000. Other newspapers estimated that it could have been as high as 100,000. Also described were the speeches and the attempts by groups of boys to disrupt the rally and speeches with bells, whistles, catcalls, shouting and stink bombs. However the event was considered to be a notable success. Among the main speakers were Emmeline and Adela Pankhurst and Nell Kenney (Bingley) and Mary Gawthorpe (Leeds).

Also described was a missed opportunity for the showmen:

"Gradually the great gathering dispersed and for a considerable time there was a very great run on the stores of refreshment houses on the Glen. Once in a way, the itinerant vendors missed a fine opportunity. Apparently they were taking their Sunday rest and did not realise what great friends they might have found in the militant suffragists and their followers."

1909 - 1913

In some years the fairs were busier than others with the vagaries of the weather and the economic situation of the country, e.g a National Coal Strike in 1912 being determinants of whether people could afford to, or wanted to visit the Glen. Easter was also becoming the most successful bank holiday of the year for those providing refreshments and entertainment.

1909 was a quiet year and 1910 saw the introduction of new proprietors who provided cinema and variety shows, harness, galloper and bicycle roundabouts and additional shooting and hoopla booths. 1911 was reported as having large crowds with the "*roundabouts and the other institutions of a usual Easter Fair reaping a rich harvest.*"

Whilst 1912 was again a quiet year, the Easter holidays in March 1913 proved to be memorable both for the weather and the size of the crowds. The Leeds Mercury of 23rd March, 1913 reported:

"*All records for Shipley Glen were easily eclipsed, the crowd being estimated to number over 100,000... the roundabouts reaped a rich harvest.*"

The Shipley Times and Express also noted:

"*On Easter Monday the Fair was extensively patronised.*"

Things were however about to change for the showmen. Rumblings of discontent had been heard at local Council level during 1913 about damage to the roads over the moor and leading to the Glen. These were to manifest themselves during 1914 as regards an announcement by Bradford Corporation.

Mechanical Apparatus Prohibited - 1914

Along with a number of other local publications, the Leeds Mercury broke the following news on 3rd April, 1914:

"*The Shipley Glen Fair has for many years been an Eastertide Institution but the Bradford Corporation which owns the Manorial Rights has come to a decision which will prevent mechanically operated fairground equipment such as heavy roundabouts and similar amusement apparatus from being installed on the Glen.*"

The resolution is intended to keep off the Glen such amusement devices as hobby horses, motor car roundabouts, joy wheels* and the like.

The chief reason for the action of the Corporation is the serious damage caused to the moorland road that was laid at considerable expense some years ago – by heavy vehicles passing over it.

Last year repairs to the road cost more than the amount received in rent from the proprietors of the amusement devices. It is assumed that there will be sufficient attractions apart from those banned to make the Glen Fair popular and enjoyable."

* Joy Wheels were a popular, short-lived, novelty ride in the early part of the last century. A polished disc in the centre of a circular wooden enclosure spun with increasing speed, gradually throwing all the riders off. The wheel was often surrounded by bench-type seats and spectators watching the action.

On the same day that the Leeds Mercury published the above article, the Shipley Times and Express also broke the news that the mechanical rides had been banned but that the stalls and shows would continue:-

"The veto to "apparatus mechanically worked" simply means that roundabouts of all descriptions from the old fashioned "hobby horses" to the modern mode of revolving motion – the motor cars – will not constitute part of the Shipley Glen Easter Fair.

Never again as we leave the higher moorlands after our annual Easter walk will the glittering lights which used to chase each other around be as tempters to a scene of gaiety. The Glen will be strangely quiet for Easter...

*For more years than one cares to remember the scene on Shipley Glen has been one of the **wonders of our local life**. The crowds who have trod the **common ground** in one day have been estimated by the hundred thousand.*

*A visit to the Glen has been properly described as the **poor man's holiday** when a trip to the seaside has not been possible. In this way it has provided **endless joys to old and young**. Municipally too it has served a big purpose for the tramway receipts have received their greatest fillip from the traffic to Saltaire at Easter.*

*...Yes stalls alone will be there we are told. But can a collection of such **minor attractions** be called a Fair? Without the roundabouts the Easter*

egg as served at Shipley Glen will not have the same taste as in former times."

Effects of the Ban in 1914

As a result of the ban, two Fairs were held at Easter 2014 and the Shipley Times and Express of 17th April, 2014 reported:

White House on the Bingley side of the Glen

"Here we find the offshoot of the original fairground. It is pushed in a grass field near the top of the Glen by the White House. I was this Tuesday not a little disappointed with the show and the crowd. Evidently it has not been the success expected. The assemblage of attractions only amounted to the total seen at many a village feast. Two or three raree shows (portable peep shows in a box), a farmyard roundabout, a motor car switchback and a few toss the ring games."

Glen Plateau

"Here on this ancient Brackenhall Green we find the Easter Fair in lively evidence. A somewhat depleted show, but not so much as might have been expected.

The lack is only with regard to the steam driven roundabouts. It was on account of the immense traction engines and the havoc they made on the moor roadways which caused the embargo from the Fair on the Glen plateau."

Natural Attractions

A third article in the same newspaper on the same date captured another angle:

"The Glen was crowded notwithstanding the exclusion of the heavy roundabouts from the Fair on the Glen plateau. The second Fair in a field on the opposite side of the Glen did not prove a success.

There is something more than the "fun of the Fair which brings the crowds to Shipley Glen at Easter."

The article then extols the virtues and benefits of the freedom of the moors, the bracing air, the charming scenery and the opportunity to escape from what it terms "the smoke-zone" of the towns.

Good Friday 1918

The First World War which had started on 28th July, 1914 and eventually finished on 11th November, 1918 had an obvious affect on all aspects of life in Britain.

In respect of the Glen, a report in the Shipley Times and Express on 5th April, 1918 effectively sums up the **possible demise** of the **area as a resort**:

"It is difficult to estimate accurately the precise causes for the change, but the contrast between the appearance of Shipley Glen on Good Friday and that which it has presented in the past was striking to a degree.

*The **removal** of the old **amusement** excrescences, the **war**, and the **weather** must all be credited with a share in producing the ultimate effect. **Instead** of the **usual crowd** the place seemed **deserted**. The attractions and amusements on the plateau- where giddy scenes were wont to be witnessed in times gone by- consisted of one ice-cream caravan, which occupies practically a permanent pitch, and a blind concertina player.*

*What a **change from the old days** of the toboggan, the aerial flight and the Royal Yorkshire Switchback!*

For nature lovers the change is all to the good and they will doubtless thank the Bradford Corporation for having initiated such a reform. Gone are the boxing saloons, the fat women shows and the screeching roundabouts. Even the milder delights of the Aunt Sallies and the sweets, trinkets and refreshment stalls were all missing yesterday.

Easter 1921

Changing tastes, the effects of war and the perennial problem of clearing up, are all identified in an article in the Shipley Times and Express of 1st April, 1921 as reasons for the **continuing demise of** the **Fair**. Whilst still **attracting** people at Bank Holidays in reasonably large numbers it was the attractions on **Prod Lane** and the **walks** on

Baildon Moor and over to **Ilkley** which became the **main draws** from this date onwards:

"Eastertide has invariably been associated with a walk over Shipley Glen. Every Easter saw Victoria Road and the various approaches to the Glen crowded with trippers, while on the Glen itself was always found a multitude of holiday makers of all ages and sexes.

Shipley Glen as a beauty spot has perennial attractions, but it was not alone the sylvan pleasures of the place which attracted the large crowds - the Glen at one time - in fact right up to the war - boasted a Fair of the real old fashioned kind.

Now however things have altered, the Fair has deteriorated. This is partly due to the fact that "young men and maidens" of the present day seem to look for higher delights than there are to be found in "innocent shies" or roundabouts and partly on account of the war. Again the costly clearing up after the Fair has resulted in the powers controlling it, limiting the number of attractions.

Once the Glen Fair had its fat men, bearded ladies, mermaids, snake charmers and fire eaters, but today its attractiveness is limited to Aunt Sally shies, cocoanut shies, a solitary roundabout and a few stalls.

Truly the glory of the Fair has departed.

Continued Patronage

Whilst the fair on the plateau effectively ceased to exist after this period, the Tramway, the Japanese Gardens, Eastells Garden Nurseries and Shipley Glen Pleasure Grounds, Old Glen House and the variety of walks all continued to be visitor attractions for many years. Some of course still exist...

4. 1930s - 2018
LOOKING BACK TO
LOOK FORWARD

Researching this book in order of chronological dates and occurrences has enabled me to make new and interesting discoveries about the Glen and its early development.

In doing so I found a retrospective article written by Harry Milner a regular contributor to the Shipley Times and Express written in 1957, in which he captured perfectly his visits to the Glen as a young child by looking back over the years, and describing what it meant to him. Perhaps his words say it all!

Victoria Road before the holiday crowds, with the Glen plateau in the background.

"I can never forget the scenes one witnessed in Saltaire. One stood on Gordon Terrace and all you could see were the continuous streams of tram cars bringing the thousands from all over with one object in view – The Glen.

Victoria Road was packed like a sardine tin and the holiday spirit was evident everywhere. As you made your way down Victoria Road you were entertained by the different vendors. I always remember the Italian lady who used to be by the canal bridge with a stand which had a bird cage on top and for a copper a small budgie would present you with a card with your fortune on.

A bit further on you came to a large crowd who were waiting to get on the Tramway to take you to the top, but we youngsters had to walk up the hill, and on the wood side it was packed with stalls of all descriptions and the crowds who were walking up to the Glen Wood were all in a good mood.

If you were lucky enough to have a ride on the Tramway through the wood you saw nature at its best. I can't think of anything nicer today than a ride on the Glen Tramway. You got to the top of the hill and Mr Wilson, the owner would be there at the gears and the old gas engine of those days would be chugging away.

When you got to the top of Glen Road you had your choice of what to do. I always used to make for Mr Hartley's Japanese Gardens on the right hand side. These gardens were always a fascination to me and I used to wonder how they made the things they had. There was a castle surrounded by water and a boat to take you round for a copper. In the greenhouse you saw all sorts of curios he had collected. His gardens were always well kept.

On the other side you had the Vulcan House Pleasure Gardens with a roundabout of cycles, swings, two donkeys walking round and round and the monkey in a cage. You went on your way to the Glen and came to the Glen House Grounds where you could have a ride on a horse drawn tram.

After leaving there you came to your object – The Glen. In those days the going was hard because we did not have a good road then as we do today. You came to the Fair and what a Fair it was. You had everything conceivable there is in the amusement world – roundabouts, shows, What the Butler Saw machines and last but not least, the Switchback on the ground adjoining Bracken Hall Farm. This Switchback stood there for years and I think it was at the Saltaire Exhibition.

Talking about Bracken Hall Farm, everyone knew the stubby little fellow who was the owner – Mr Marsden. He was always clad in his knickerbockers, with his Norfolk jacket and deerstalking hat. I shall always remember the rustic work he had made in his front garden with its tea tables, where you got a good cup of tea.

The holidaymakers who did not want the fair travelled further afield to Dick Hudson's. The crowds that used to congregate at this hostelry were really marvellous. I think that 99 out of every 100 who had a meal there had ham and eggs. The landlord was famed for his home cured ham. You entered the hotel and there were the hams hung up on hooks in the ceiling and the smell of the ham cooking whetted your appetite.

After a short rest you could either go forward to Ilkley or walk over to The Hermit at Burley Woodhead."

Nostalgia at Easter

In similar vein an article in the Target in 1985 captured nostalgic early memories for Rebecca Baldwin who was born in Saltaire and was lucky to have the Glen on her doorstep as a playground.

"People came from miles around to visit the place. For them it was a special outing – every bit as good as a trip to the coast which few people could afford in those days."

Her most vivid memories were of Easter - the annual red letter day on the Glen.

"A queue of trams would unload their passengers at the top of Victoria Road and it was just one great sea of heads all going one way – to the Glen."

Rebecca's earliest recollections were riding up the **Glen Tramway** on the shoulders of her elder brother who was later killed in the First World War. She particularly remembered the masses of **bluebells** alongside the railway and the stalls selling penny walking sticks, brandy snap and penny ice cream cornets.

Once up on Prod Lane she remembered that her greatest thrill was a ride on the aerial runway in the **Pleasure Grounds**, known as the **Cape to Cairo railway**. However she never dared ride on the **Switchback** further up the Glen as it was too hair raising. Other memorable treats were penny donkey rides and a ride on the *boat* in the *Japanese Gardens*. *"Mr Hartley who ran it used to call out "three times round the world for a penny"! What value you got for a penny in those days!"*

Yorkshire Film Archive

The following link: www.yorkshirefilmarchive.com/film/easter-shipley-glen-1912 shows a silent film of images from Easter Monday 1912 on Shipley Glen.

Short and Laister (2003) provide a context and written commentary and the film itself captures the sheer scale of the number of visitors visiting the Glen and the flavour of what Harry Milner and Rebecca Baldwin described.

Featured are the **Trams, Victoria Road, Glen Tramway, Switchback, Glen plateau, Fairground roundabouts, amusements, rides and games**.

As an additional resource, the film is well worth viewing, as it provides an invaluable pictorial reference point and images which complement the context and content of this book.

1930s to 1990s

Whilst this book concentrates on the Victorian/ Edwardian period of development of the Glen there are of course many people who have experienced the Glen in later years. To capture some of those moments, in the **next section photographs from the 1930s until the 1990s are shown as pictorial memories of each decade**.

1930s

Easter on the Glen Plateau (1938).
Courtesy of Telegraph & Argus.

Whilst the Fair as it had once been no longer existed the Glen was still a destination at Easter. Refreshment and games stalls were still set up on the plateau as the photograph on the previous page shows. In the background the Old Glen House advertises teas.

Additionally, people still used the Glen as a starting point to reach Dick Hudson's. Brown (1931) in *Moorland Tramping in Yorkshire*, comments:

"Who does not remember their first walk over Shipley Glen to Dick Hudson's - that half-way inn whose ham and eggs have been famous throughout the West Riding these forty years."

1940s

The photograph below shows a small steam locomotive built by D. Graham of Baildon, which could haul twelve adults in the Japanese Gardens. It was reported that between 1946 and 1948 the locomotive had hauled 20,000 people.

A Model Train at the Japanese Gardens in the 1940s.

1950s

Madge Raistrick owned and ran the Old Glen House from 1948 as a restaraunt, cafe and tearoom, until she retired in 1983. She also bred peacocks which became a novelty attraction as they strutted round the gardens. On her retirement a local development company bought the premises and restored it, converting the interior into a liscensed hotel and restaurant. Nowadays it is run as a pub and restaraunt run by Ed Ward and Louise Harrison.

Peacocks at the Old Glen House Tearooms and Restaurant.
Courtesy of Telegraph & Argus.

1960s

The photograph below of the Glen plateau captures perfectly the more "laid back" attitude that many people associate with the 1960s. The Old Glen in the background still advertises Teas.

The Glen Plateau (1969).   *Courtesy of Telegraph & Argus.*

1970s

The Shipley Glen Tramway (photograph opposite taken in 1979) has seen a number of changes of ownership and administration over the years. As previously stated, the Woodheads owned it until 1928. Herbert and Patti Parr then ran it until 1942. In 1943 five businessmen under the auspices of **Glen Tramways Limited** took over the business and initially employed George Rushton as Manager until the late 1950s. Shipley Urban District Council were now owners of the land. which they indicated they wanted to clear. They were eventually succeeded by **Bradford Metropolitan Council.**

Local business people including Paul Teale owner of the Pleasure Grounds and the Parkinson family who operated the Japanese Gardens for a time, ensured that the Tramway continued through the formation of **Glen Enterprises Limited**. It now became a part-time business which Glen Enterprises ran until early 1981, when because of trading difficulties they handed over the Tramway to the Council.

In January 1982 the Telegraph and Argus announced that the **Bradford Trolleybus Association** (BTA), a group of enthusiasts, would restore and operate the Tranway, assisted by a grant from Bradford Council to help with restoration costs. **Mick Leak** records that until 1994 , the Tramway was entirely staffed by unpaid BTA volunteers. From that year and with the backing of supporters, the lease was transferred to Mick and his wife Maureen, with the BTA acting as Friends of the Glen Tramway - "*still all unpaid.*"

Mick and his wife ran the tramway from 1994 until 2002 when they surrendered the lease in the Autumn of that year. They continued to operate the line and train volunteers into the early months of 2003. From then until November, Mick was involved in maintenance and drawing up of Instruction Manuals until they left to live in Eire in December 2003.

In 2002 **The Glen Tramway Preservation Company Limited a Trust** with **charitable status** was formed under a lease from, and with the full backing of Bradford Council. The Tramway is now run by Trustees and a team of volunteers.

Shipley Glen Tramway.   *Courtesy of Telegraph & Argus.*

1980s

Bracken Hall Countryside Centre shown below was opened on the 31st May 1981 by Mari and John Friend with help from the Bradford Countryside Service and the Countryside Commission. The Centre contained information on the ecology and history of the Glen as well as the immediate surrounding area. It also originally housed observation aquariums where visitors could view the lifecycles of bees, dragonfly nymphs, water spiders, newts, sticklebacks and other small animals. From 1984 the Centre was run by City of Bradford Metropolitan District Council and since 2015 by the Friends of Bracken Hall Countryside Centre.

Bracken Hall Countryside Centre (1987).
Courtesy of Telegraph & Argus.

1990s

The 1990s were the last decade in which the sign shown below would be relevant. The dodgems shown opposite closed in the mid/late 1990s and the Shipley Glen Pleasure Grounds and Funfair also shown below closed in September 2005.

Signage to Shipley Glen.   *Courtesy of Telegraph & Argus.*

Courtesy of Mike Lawson.

The Wysocki family ran the dodgems for a number of years. The vintage dodgems shown above were eventually replaced by new ones. The dodgems and the Glen Tramway were used as backdrops in the TV movie Blood and Peaches released in 1995.

2018

The next section describes the hopes and aspirations of the individuals and volunteers who still run businesses or attractions on Shipley Glen in 2018.

LOOKING FORWARD

This section describes the hopes and aspirations of some of the individuals and volunteers who still run businesses or attractions on Shipley Glen.

Nowadays besides the wide open spaces that are still the Glen and of course the road over to Eldwick and up to Dick Hudsons and the walk to Ilkley, little remains of what Harry Milner described on page 100.

Amongst the attractions which still exist are the Glen Tramway, run by volunteers, the Old Glen House pub and Old Glen Tearooms run as separate businesses, Bracken Hall House and Farm run as businesses and Bracken Hall Countryside Centre, also run by volunteers.

What also exists of course are the memories of individuals and families who have lived on the Glen or visited it over the years, right up to present times.

As a sequel to the last section of this book I'd like to give the businesses/ voluntary bodies which still exist, the opportunity to celebrate their continued existence with a comment on their hopes and aspirations for the future...

Shipley Glen Tramway

The Tramway is a **Registered Charity** and run entirely by **volunteers**. It is a cable hauled funicular tramway and the Trustees have 125 year lease expiring in 2126 from Bradford Metropolitan District Council.

The Tramway Trustees have a **responsibility** which they willingly accept now and for the future for the **upkeep and improvement of the tramway tracks, trams and buildings**, bearing in mind to maintain the **traditional appearance** of the Tramway in keeping with its 1895 opening in the late **Victorian** era by **Sam Wilson**. **Increasing fund raising** and **passenger income** is a **key** to the **future success** of Shipley Glen Tramway along with **volunteer recruitment and training**.

Trustees and volunteers intend to **expand the role of Shipley Glen Tramway** with local schools and groups for visits to use the **displays** on **historical** and **social history** of Shipley **Glen Tramway, Shipley Glen** and **Saltaire** in the newly built **information centre** at the tramway bottom station and also to allow all **visitors** to **enjoy** a **ride** on the **trams**.

Richard Freeman - Trustee

Old Glen House

The Old Glen House Pub has been part of the **community** for **many years** and in the 4.5 years Louise and myself have run the pub it is something we are very much **trying to continue**. The pub is a **family/ dog friendly** pub with a warm welcome offered to everyone and their four legged friends and is something our staff fully embraces.

Our objective when we took over was to try and create a **traditional** pub feel with traditional values but also move with the times and **embrace the future**.

We have built a brilliant **customer base**, which includes **locals, families, dog walkers, mountain bikers, climbers, horse riders** and walkers, **young and old,** all the things that are made possible on the beautiful Shipley Glen.

Serving a wide variety of home cooked fresh food, cask ales, lagers and fine wines in a **comfortable** and safe environment allowing people to **relax** and have a laugh and create **memories**.

We hope to continue to provide a place where people feel **welcome** and part of the pub, listening to what people want and hopefully providing a place that in the future continues to build a **business** that **embraces** the surroundings and the **community**, supporting local **groups, charities and business**.

Having personally made some great friends since taking over the pub it has become a lifestyle for Louise & myself and we both look forward to many more years in such a great pub in such an **amazing location**.

Ed Ward and Louise Harrison - Licensees

Tea-room

My name is Peter Grubisic and I'm a **locally born** Shipley, West Yorkshire lad. I have **known the Glen** and Baildon Moor all my life and have been there **countless times** with **family** and **friends** in my **early youth**.

Recently I had the **opportunity** to **buy The Old Glen Tearooms** and I jumped at it. It's not until now that I have realised the **graceful beauty** of the Glen and Baildon Moor and the long **fascinating history** connected to it. If I could shout out to the whole world and tell them what they are missing by not visiting the Glen and the moor and looking into its long standing history, I would.

It offers possibly one of the greatest **family accessible** locations in the area. **Fascinating** and **beautiful** is not enough to describe it. **Mind blowing** comes to mind.

Peter Grubisic - Owner

Bracken Hall House

We have lovingly converted the **period property** on Bracken Hall Green (Shipley Glen) into a **luxury 5* B&B**, not just because we happened to notice there was no such bespoke accommodation nearby, but because we have **strong family connections** with the area. The Illingworth family have **farmed here for over 50 years** and we believe the whole area around **Shipley Glen** and **Bracken Hall** is **special**, **steeped** in **history** and requires **preserving**. We have created a business close to family whilst pursuing a lifestyle change and are also proud that **Bracken Hall Countryside Centre** has been **saved from closure** (by carefully ensuring our plans included this **community element**).

Due to our **links** with **Bracken Hall** and a genuine interest in the area we are able to provide our guests with **specific local knowledge** and expertise and are **attracting new guests to Bracken Hall** from all over the world! It is also great when guests who stay at the B&B **share** their own **personal memories of growing up or visiting Shipley Glen**. We often share **old photographs** and provide **historical information** but now, thanks to **Alan,** we can offer them a book dedicated to the local history!

We have plans for the **business to grow & diversify** whilst keeping **luxury B&B** and **local tourism** at its heart. We already have bookings throughout 2018 with specific groups seeking to hire the whole of Bracken Hall House out on a **self-catering** basis, thus allowing people to stay longer to **explore** everything this **area** has to offer. The feedback from guests so far has been so positive and they are returning again and again.

It is fantastic to **look back** and '**take a peek**' into the **history of Shipley Glen,** especially the amazing **photographic evidence** of entrepreneurs gone by. What is also quite astounding is how only a small part of those historical attractions physically remain intact **and how nature has taken back 'The Glen'.** We are secretly pleased that 'The Glen' has returned to a **peaceful, tranquil place to escape the hustle and bustle of city life.**

Sally and Stuart Illingworth

Bracken Hall Countryside Centre

The Bracken Hall Countryside Centre has been an important attraction since it **first opened** in **1981.** The vision of **Mari and John Friend,** the Centre originally occupied a **converted café/ice cream parlour and family garden.** A change of ownership led to major reworking and a new building in the mid-'80s and eventually to it becoming one of Bradford's museums. Now in its **third incarnation,** after Bradford Council closed it in 2013, the Centre exists through the **generous support of Sally and Stuart Illingworth,** the property's current owners, and a **dedicated band of volunteers.** It is funded by **Baildon Town Council,** by **educational group visits, hire** for third-party functions, and by **public donations.**

People love to come back to the Glen and to the Centre. Many of our **visitors first came as children,** often on school trips, and now come along with their **own children**. **Grandparents** bring their **grandchildren** and share experiences that they had with their **own children**. Many **families** have become **regular visitors**, appreciating the special events and educational and crafting opportunities the Centre provides. For its general opening, the **wildlife garden's upkeep**, and for **many events**, **activities**, **guided walks** and **displays**, the Centre is largely dependent on a diverse collective of **volunteers** and their energy. Indeed, the **Friends of Bracken Hall Countryside Centre** were crucial in the Centre's survival and its continued popularity. **New volunteers** are always **welcome**.

As well as adapting to its new circumstances, Bracken Hall is also embracing the **changing pressures** placed on the **countryside** in recent years. This is keeping the place fresh whilst building on its core values, allowing it to **actively engage** with its **visitors** and further develop its role as a **community asset**. The Centre is an essential part of the broader Shipley Glen "experience", promoting the area and co-developing events, trails and facilities with other local attractions and businesses.

Richard White - Bracken Hall Countryside Centre Manager

LOOKING BACK ON LOOKING BACK - A RETROSPECTIVE SUMMARY

I started my research and writing journey for this book considering that I had a good knowledge of the development of Shipley Glen, having researched and written about it before.

Using internet sources I discovered that there is a greater and expanding range of information available than previously, particularly through sources such as the British Newspaper Archives. My recent research has given me access to more detailed sources than I expected when I began. Consequently I have been able to make links in the story of Shipley Glen that perhaps were not available to previous researchers.

Victorian/Edwardian Entertainment

There are several texts which have sought to identify Victorian/Edwardian venues and entertainments as either **pleasure gardens, pleasure parks/pleasure grounds or amusement parks**. These sources are identified in the Bibliography to this book.

To develop my own understanding and in order to appreciate the influences that shaped the entertainments on the Glen, I also sought the historical development and definition of the above.

Historical Development

Below are the names of some of the principal venues and type which influenced the direction of entertainment in Victorian and Edwardian times:

Vauxhall - UK - 1732 - Pleasure Gardens

Tivoli Gardens - Denmark - 1843 - Pleasure Gardens and then an Amusement Park

Coney Island - USA - 1880 - Amusement Park

Blackpool Pleasure Beach - 1896 - Amusement Park

The Kursaal - UK - 1901 Southend Marine Park and Gardens

Definition

- **Pleasure Garden** - A garden open to the public for recreation and entertainment. Pleasure Gardens differ from other public gardens by serving as venues for music, entertainment and attractions such as bandstands, amusement rides, zoos and menageries and tea rooms.

- **Amusement Park** - A park that features various attractions such as rides and games as well as other events for entertainment purposes. An open-air area consisting of stalls, side shows etc or a large park equipped with recreational devices such as merry-go-rounds, roller coasters and usually also having booths for games and refreshments.

- **Pleasure Grounds** - Commons, a piece of land for recreational use. As industrial cities grew in density, land often at the edge of a town was used as pleasure grounds, intended as a public health benefit. Some pleasure grounds contained commercially opened areas with stalls and shows for amusement as well as funfairs and rides.

- **Playground** - An area where many people go for recreation.

The Glen - An Enigma

However none of the Bibliography sources seem to identify exactly what Shipley Glen was, although a couple of them identify it as a "crossover site" which bridged the gap between the late pleasure gardens and the first amusement parks. In reality it was probably all those things. You may ask yourself...does that really matter?

Essentially the Glen was about **people's expectations**. In the Victorian age new and novel ideas were being introduced in commerce and industry, and also in **entertainment**. If you spent most of your week at work in an **unhealthy environment** and **lived** in an industrialised and **smoke ridden** area, of course you wanted to escape to somewhere where there was a sense of **healthy** living, **freedom**, excitement and **adventure**.

The Glen was therefore **different things** to **different people**, at **different times**. Difficult to put a name or definition to...

Namely **open common land**. A place where teetotal groups and Sunday schools could picnic or obtain refreshment and teas. A place of **peace and tranquillity**. A busy and **energetic fairground**. A venue for **thrilling rides**. A place to start your **walk across the moors. Legislation** dictated how it was used. **Ownership** of the Glen also dictated how it was used. Local **residents** had to **tolerate** regular **invasions** of where they lived, some started their own small businesses to cater for visitors. **Speculators** attempted to make **money** out of **ventures** on the Glen. **Unfenced or enclosed. Without** public **facilities** and **gas or electric energy. Difficult to manage** as a **commercial activity** because of the **individual interests** of the many entertainment providers.

All these things shaped the development of the Glen and that is why it was difficult to identify what the Glen was or was not.

Conlin (2012 pp227) states *"Part of the problem that scholars have faced in trying to pin down where amusement parks came from is that they brought together multiple types of entertainment in or near an outside space."*

In seeking a title for this book I called the Glen a **playground** rather than a **pleasure ground/park or amusement park**. It was **what it was** because of **where it was** and was **unique** in the range of activities it provided over time. It was primarily **defined by who used it**.

If you describe a place as a playground for a certain group of people you mean that those people like to enjoy themselves or go on holiday there...such as **St Tropez - a playground for the rich and famous...** or **Shipley Glen - a playground for the Victorian working classes**. People went there essentially to **play** and **escape** from the rigours and confines of hard work, unhealthy living and a fairly humdrum existence.

Sadly, nowadays the Glen seems to some people strangely **deserted** compared to how it once was. To others it has **returned to how it was in the first place**, having taken hundreds of thousands of people on a **journey** with it.

Not the Only Place

Taylor (1986 pp179) observes:

*"One of the features of **West Riding leisure life** which has **virtually ceased to exist** is the Pleasure Park, popular in late Victorian and Edwardian times and even up to the outbreak of the Second World War. Only **three** remain out of a **former twelve**, and they are far from being typical of the genre. Roundhay Park, Leeds, and Lister Park, Bradford, are municipally owned, and **Shipley Glen is more of a complex made up of several businesses and attractions owned by different people.**" (Now however these have closed down apart from the Glen Tramway.)*

Taylor also identified what he thought was the perfect ending to a day on the Glen, which as a metaphor also sadly signals not only the end of a day, but also the demise of an era of simple pleasures:

*"On Prod Lane another popular feature of the Glen, the Glen Nurseries was started by William Eastell in the 1930s...**Visits to Shipley Glen would often end with a bunch of flowers, a plant or some tomatoes to take home.**"*

...it is not difficult to advance reasons for the demise of the pleasure park – more and more individual transport with individual affluence and the possibility of extended outings, changing social habits and foreign holidays with consequent wider horizons.

Social circumstances and expectations changed over time which is the reason that the Glen as it was no longer exists.

Nostalgia and Enchantment

Jane Fielder's painting as a cover to this book set a pictorial context to the text. Her words as an adult and grandparent also seem to capture a sense of enchantment when she observes:

A Magical Place, Shipley Glen

*"Whenever my brother, Ian and his family visit, one of the first things Ian always says is "Can we go to Shipley Glen, I want to **check that it was real and not a dream.**" It has that affect on people. **It is such a magical, enchanted place.***

Back in the early 1980's, we used to regularly visit the glen with our three small boys. They loved walking through the woods from Gilstead and emerging at the back of the Old Glen Pub and tea rooms. We'd stop for an ice cream and they'd be bursting to get to the amusements. They were amazing. The aerial glide was their favourite, but the dodgems and slot machines were a close second.

*Then on to the **tramway**. What a magnificent **treasure**. Smiley, willing helpers, wonderful sweets and the brilliant ride itself. It brings back such **happy memories**.*

*I still love it today, though sadly the fairground has gone, and **return again and again** with my **grandchildren** now!"*

Taylor (1986 pp179) also mirrors this in his nostalgic and perceptive thought about Pleasure Parks/Grounds, which is perhaps a fitting end to this book:

"Our enjoyment was probably heightened because we visited them in childhood or adolescence when judgement was not too sophisticated or matured by experience. Distance - in time - too probably leads to enchantment."

5. SHIPLEY GLEN CHRONOLOGICAL TIMELINE – 1846 – 1921

5/9/1846	Lincolnshire Chronicle – Bradford Railway Station three months old...Every day scores of passengers take a ride to get a country walk or picnic at Eldwick Glen.
1850	Charles Clegg Converted Wood Head Farm into a Temperance Hotel.
15/4/1852	Bradford Observer. Eldwick Glen. This favourite retreat of pleasure seekers has since Friday last been visited by thousands of persons of both sexes. On Good Friday there was a constant stream of people pouring to and from the Glen during the afternoon. Though a considerable distance from the town the holiday folk have made this distant place a scene of great enjoyment and the desire which has been thus exhibited by our population for rural and outdoor recreations, which we trust stimulate the friends of the Park Movement to renew efforts to place the means of such harmless enjoyment within easy and almost daily access.
21/7/1853	Bradford Observer. Eldwick Glen Sunday School festivity for 200 children from Lightcliffe, Halifax The trip and refreshments were provided by Titus Salt and included a day at Eldwick Glen where Titus and personal friends mingled.
23/7/1853	Leeds Times – Shipley Glen little known.
23/7/1853	Leeds Times. In the Glen there is an excellent house for refreshment known as the British Temperance Hotel and kept by Mr W. Cooper and has been occupied by him and his ancestors for over two

centuries. It is a curious antique building supposed to be upwards of 400 years old, has no ceiling whilst the immense rafters and thatch are very prominent to the eye.

29/4/1854	Leeds Times. Accommodation at Abraham Whiteheads Broadstones House - Tea, Coffee and Snacks - Sunday School Scholars accommodated.
30/4/1857	Bradford Observer. Saltaire Essay and Debating Society 60 members, dancing, games and tea provided by Mr A. Whitehead.
7/1/1858	Bradford Observer. Christmas Rambles - Fleece Inn, Hudson.
22/9/1858	Bradford Observer. 5th Anniversary opening of Saltaire mill. At noon workforce and two bands proceeded to Eldwick Glen where dancing and other outdoor recreations pleasantly wiled away a few hours of the fine sunny afternoon.
2/6/1860	Leeds Intelligencer. Teachers and School - Church Trip.
27/6/1861	Bradford Observer. Sunday School Trips.
15/8/1863	Leeds Times. Church Trip.
13/8/1864	Preston Herald. Un-enfranchised Radical Reformers Working Men's Political Picnic.
3/6/1865	Leeds Times. Grand Gala's in Mr Cleggs Pleasure Garden Whit Mon and Tues.
5/4/1866	Leeds Mercury. Working Men's Reform Government Franchise Meeting.
5/4/1866	Bradford Observer. Changing face of Shipley Glen mill workers visits.
25/4/1867	Bradford Observer. Reform Demonstration.
16/4/1868	Bradford Observer. Shipley Glen becoming popular at Easter as a place of amusement and recreation. Saltaire, Bingley and Shipley Brass Bands dance and other music. Charles Clegg, Caterer is mentioned.

14/6/1868	Bradford Observer. Wesleyan Sunday School meeting, 800 pupils had tea in a large marquee in a field lent by Mr Charles Clegg of the Glen, Baildon.
22/3/1869	Bradford Observer. Grand Gala and Brass Band at Shipley Glen, Good Friday at Mr Walkers field.
8/5/1869	Leeds Times. Half day Trip to Shipley Glen on Midland Rail.
19/5/1869	Yorkshire Post and Leeds Intelligencer. Shipley Glen busy.
29/9/1869	Bradford Daily Telegraph. 65 Inmates of Skipton Workhouse visit Shipley Glen and tea at Mr Whiteheads Temperance Hotel.
30/3/1870	Leeds Mercury. Rally by Working Men of Bradford and Education Bill.
11/4/1870	Bradford Observer. Tea at Charles Cleggs, Shipley Glen.
21/4/1870	Bradford Observer. Whiteheads Temperance Hotel - Stalls and Dancing Broadstone House.
8/6/1870	Bradford Observer. Scholars and Sunday School Visits and picnic parties - Mr Walkers Field.
1871	Bank Holidays Act introduced.
8/4/1871	Bradford Observer. Opening of Season on Shipley Glen - Stalls etc. Estimated 10,000 visitors.
21/5/1872	Bradford Daily Telegraph. Sunday schools trip. Enterprising individual has erected a refreshment premises.
15/6/1872	Leeds Times. Leeds Band of Hope Grand Trip to Shipley Glen.
10/8/1872	Yorkshire Post and Leeds Intelligencer. Scientific walk, tea at British Temperance and Coffee House.
12/4/1873	Bradford Observer. Shipley Glen Fair.
28/7/1873	Huddersfield Chronicle. Teachers trip to Shipley Glen.

1874	School teachers and scholars trips to Shipley Glen.
9/4/1874	Bradford Observer. Easter - more tickets to Shipley Glen than ever before 35,000 tickets.
29/8/1874	Huddersfield Chronicle. Sunday Schools Tea provided at Broadstones House.
4/2/1875	Bradford Observer. British Temperance Hotel - Famous resort in Spring and Summer months. 20 years ago newly discovered spot known to only those living near.
18/5/1875	Bradford Observer. Quiet - Church groups and Sunday Schools.
19/6/1875	Leeds Times. Leeds and District Band of Hope trip to Saltaire and Shipley Glen.
1875	Charles Clegg left Glen House.
1876	William Wade Maude inherited the title of Lord of the Manor of Baildon on the death of Abraham, his father.
14/1/1876	Hull Packet. Letter recommending - 7 miles from Saltaire over Rombalds Moor to Ilkley.
9/3/1876	Bradford Observer. Gambling at Shipley Glen.
15/4/1876	Bradford Observer. Shipley and Saltaire Brass Bands - 30 - 40,000 visitors.
6/6/76	Bradford Daily Telegraph. Refreshment houses busy- outside amusements the same.
22/7/1876	Yorkshire Post and Leeds Intelligencer. Half day visits and cheap weekend return tickets.
31/3/1877	Bradford Observer. Brass Bands and other attractions. Broadstone House off Sherrif Lane near Shipley Glen.
14/7/1877	Shipley Times and Express. Primitive Methodists Band of Hope visit. Tea and games at Mr Walker's.
16/7/1877	Bradford Observer. York Naturalists Union visit.

20/4/1878	Bradford Observer. Notice from Maude, Lord of the Manor, no stalls or Fair apparatus - but were allowed on payment of a small fee. Formal assertion of Manorial Rights.
17/3/1879	Shipley Times and Express. Grand Easter Gala - Shipley Brass Band.
12/4/1879	Leeds Mercury. 45 - 50,000 at Fair - largest ever.
22/7/1879	Bradford Observer. Old Glen House auction.
22/8/1879	Huddersfield Chronicle. Chapel visits.
1879	Vulcan House Built.
27/3/1880	Shipley Times and Express. W. Denby - Teas - New Scarborough, Shipley Glen.
11/5/1880	Bradford Daily Telegraph. Old Glen House Tea and Strawberry Gardens - James P. Dewhurst.
16/7/1881	Leeds Times. Bradford Band of Hope and Temperance Society - tea at Old Glen House.
27/8/1881	Shipley Times and Express. Application to Otley Magistrates for a Licence to sell Alcohol by J. P. Dewirst of Old Glen House. Licence refused.
3/6/1882	Shipley Times and Express. Stalls and Fair.
28/7/1882	Todmorden and District News. Luddenden Sunday School trip.
9/9/1882	Shipley Times and Express. Circular tram open and running at Old Glen House.
2/12/1882	Shipley Times and Express. Old Glen House - Large Room with Piano.
17/3/1883	Shipley Times and Express. Shipley Glen Tram Cars now running.
27/1/1883	Large room with piano for private parties. Old Glen House.
31/3/1883	Shipley Times and Express. 20,000 visit Shipley Glen.
19/3/1883	Bradford Daily Telegraph. Set of Steam Velocipedes,

	Organ and Wagon for sale. Can be seen at New Scarborough, Shipley Glen.
28/4/1883	Shipley Times and Express. Allsop's Photographic Album and Paintings of Saltaire and Shipley Glen.
10/8/1883	Bradford Daily Telegraph. Visit by Practical Naturalists Society.
10/8/1883	Todmorden Advertiser and Hebden Bridge Newsletter. Walden Methodist Choir visit.
12/4/1884	Shipley Times and Express. Easter - Evidence of Swings, Roundabouts and Knock 'em Downs. 30,000 visitors in one day.
27/6/1884	Huddersfield Chronicle. Huddersfield Wesleyan Band of Hope tea at Old Glen House.
8/8/1884	Wharfedale and Airedale Observer. Wesleyan Methodists open air camp.
1885	Old Cruck House/Temperance Tearooms were demolished. Shipley Times and Express article of 20/2/1886 titled Gleanings of Eldwick Glen and its Surroundings confirms the demolition date of 1885.
4/4/1885	Bradford Daily Telegraph. Numerous visitors at Easter.
4/8/1885	Bradford Daily Telegraph. Shipley Glen had its usual thousands of pleasure seekers.
24/4/1886	Leeds Mercury. Popularity of Shipley Glen continues to increase and more people visited than in any previous year. Plateau completely covered with people.
27/8/1886	Bradford Daily Telegraph. Increasing numbers of visitors. 15,000 in one day.
9/10/1886	Shipley Times and Express. Birds eye view of Proposed Royal Jubilee Exhibition Grounds at Saltaire.
9/4/1887	Bradford Daily Telegraph. Large numbers at Shipley Glen.
6/5/1887	Leeds Mercury - The Royal Yorkshire Jubilee Exhibition.

28/5/1887	Yorkshire Post and Leeds Intelligencer. Toboggan erected at Exhibition by Brown and Backhouse of Liverpool - description of size.
4/6/1887	Shipley Times and Express. Saltaire Exhibition overshadowed everything else but it goes without saying that Shipley Glen was the rendezvous of many.
25/6/1887	Leeds Mercury. Switchback stands alongside toboggan at Exhibition.
1/7/1887	Wharfedale and Airedale Observer. Construction of switchback at Exhibition.
9/8/1887	Bradford Daily Telegraph. Employers tea at Old Glen House.
27/12/1887	Leeds Mercury - Sale of a Camera Obscura from Royal Yorkshire Jubilee Exhibition.
7/1/1888	Leeds Times. Samuel Bentley - Shipley Glen Refreshment Room.
3/4/1888	Yorkshire Post and Leeds Intelligencer. On the plateau of Shipley Glen a favourite attraction was the Switchback Railway which lately occupied a place in the Saltaire Exhibition Grounds. Numerous miscellaneous stalls.
7/4/1888	Shipley Times and Express. On Shipley Glen the itinerant showmen and refreshment caterers had the plateau to themselves while the Switchback Railway which has lately been transferred to the summit of the Glen by some Baildon amusement speculators was almost unpatronised.
10/7/1888	Bradford Daily Telegraph. Bradford Temperance Band of Hope annual trip to Shipley Glen.
30/7/1888	Huddersfield Chronicle. Girls Friendly Society dinner at Old Glen House arranged by Mr Dewhurst in a large room.

24/8/1888	Wharfedale and Airedale Observer. Girlington Band of Hope visit mentions swings and Switchback Railway.
1/12/1888	York Herald. Jane, wife of JW Perry of Vulcan House dies.
1889	Aerial Flight built by Halliday and Badland - great attraction.
23/3/1889	Shipley Times and Express. Complaint about Aerial Flight - Commons Preservation Society.
30/3/1889	Shipley Times and Express. Aerial Flight. Commons Preservation Society.
17/4/1889	Yorkshire Post and Leeds Intelligencer. Amalgamated Co of Showmen and Amusement Caterers, Collecting tolls - Permission from Maude to let portions of the moor for Easter and Whitsun - Commons rights, Commons Preservation Society.
20/4/1889	Shipley Times and Express. Test of ropes and cars on Aerial Flight made by Mr W. B. Woodhead - satisfactory (page 8).
20/4/1889	Shipley Times and Express. Members of Aerial Flight Co - William Wade Maude, Halliday, Mark Badland etc (page 7).
27/4/1889	Leeds Times. 30,000 visititors - Aerial Flight an attraction.
27/4/1889	Shipley Times and Express. Good Friday accident - woman fell 40 feet from Aerial Flight platform.
15/6/1889	Shipley Times and Express. Aerial Flight - Switchback, showmen, stall owners, very quiet.
15/6/1889	Shipley Times and Express. Large Salvation Army picnic on Shipley Glen.
8/4/1890	Leeds Mercury. Alcoholic drinks legally sold by a caterer in a field near the plateau for first time since the Glen became a holiday resort.

11/4/1890	Wharfedale and Airedale Observer. Glen very busy and swarming with visitors. Fair, shows, Aerial Flight and Switchback very busy.
30/6/1890	Bradford Daily Telegraph. Meeting and tea for Smiths and Farriers Society at Vulcan House.
31/3/1891	Leeds Mercury. Manningham Mills Strike Demo at Shipley Glen.
4/4/1891	Shipley Times and Express. Switchback, Aerial Flight and itinerant showmen, brisk business - "a veritable fairground." Manorial Rights, speculators mentioned.
9/5/1991	Yorkshire Post and Leeds Intelligencer. Number of visitors large.
4/8/1891	Leeds Mercury. Glen very busy with thousands of visitors.
24/3/1892	Yorkshire Evening Post. For stands for refreshments and amusements on Shipley Glen during Good Friday and Easter Monday, Apply Manor Bailiff, The Park, Baildon.
8/5/1893	Yorkshire Post and Leeds Intelligencer. Bradford Independent Labour party. Attendance estimated at being 10 - 20,000.
18/2/1893	Bradford Daily Telegraph. Colonel Maude's rights to sell Shipley Glen.
25/2/1893	Shipley Times and Express. meeting of freeholders. Manorial rights.
4/4/1893	Leeds Mercury. Large numbers at the Glen.
31/3/1894	Shipley Times and Express. Easter estimated 50 - 100,000.
19/5/1894	Shipley Times and Express. Great many people visited. Switchback and Aerial Flight largely patronised.
7/8/1994	Bradford Daily Telegraph. Great many visitors.
24/11/1894	Shipley Times and Express. Plans for wire rope railway submitted by Sam Wilson to Baildon Local Board.

1/12/1894	Shipley Times and Express The Proposed Railway up Shipley Glen Wood - Plans approved.
1895	ILP meeting near Aerial Flight.
6/4/1895	Shipley Times and Express. Preservation of Shipley Glen - Maude and Brad Corporation.
13/4/1895	Shipley Times and Express. Tramway opening delayed.
20/4/1895	Shipley Times and Express. Eastertide visitors numerous fair, rides and shows very busy. Discussion of new roads to the area.
17/5/1895	Shipley Times and Express. Trial run of Tramway.
18/5/1895	Shipley Times and Express. Glen Tramway opened.
11/5/1895	Shipley Times and Express. Bradford Independent Labour Party meeting.
7/4/1896	Yorkshire Post and Leeds Intelligencer. Easter - Larger numbers than ever.
4/6/1896	Leeds Mercury. Large number of holiday makers.
29/6/1896	Huddersfield Chronicle. Wesleyan Chapel Choir visit. Rode on new Glen tramway, had tea at Old Glen House, then rode on the Switchback and Aerial Flight.
6/8/1896	Leeds Mercury. New tramway unable to carry all passengers. Switchback and Aerial Flight popular and refreshment houses busy.
20/2/1897	Shipley Times and Express. Toboggan Slide Plan to Baildon Council.
17/4/1897	Leeds Times. Toboggan slide objection letter.
21/8/1897	Leeds Mercury. Conference - Acquisition of Shipley Glen by Bradford Corporation.
18/11/1997	Yorkshire Post and Leeds Intelligencer. Proposed purchase of Shipley Glen.
1898	Toboggan run built by Sam Wilson.
11/4/1898	Leeds Mercury. Shipley Glen visited by many thousands.

10/5/1898	Yorkshire Evening Post. Proposal to sell Shipley Glen.
17/11/1898	Bradford Daily Telegraph. Purchase of Shipley Glen.
4/4/1899	Bradford Daily Telegraph. Bradford Midland Station besieged by crowds going to Shipley Glen.
13/5/1899	Shipley Times and Express. Bradford Labour Day demonstration.
15/7/1899	Shipley Times and Express. School Visit. Tea served at Old Glen House by Mr Dewhirst.
12/8/1899	Shipley Times and Express. August Bank holiday crowds quite large.
13/1/1900	Shipley Times and Express. Award to waiter for damage to suit on toboggan ride.
17/4/1900	Bradford Daily Telegraph. Easter - Shipley Glen rapidly invaded.
29/5/1900	Bradford Daily Telegraph Bradford Corporation inspection re better government of the Glen.
6/6/1900	Yorkshire Evening Post. Toboggan accident.
7/9/1900	Yorkshire Post and Leeds Intelligencer. Notice to remove Aerial Flight and toboggan.
15/9 1900	Shipley Times and Express. Dismantling of Aerial Flight and toboggan.
17/11/1900	Yorkshire Post and Leeds Intelligencer. Auction of all the woodwork for the Toboggan and Aerial Flight.
9/4/1901	Bradford Observer. Switchback and itinerant vendors busy.
29/5/1901	Bradford Observer. Great number of holidaymakers.
15/6/1901	Bradford Observer. Notice of Sale of Aerial Flight.
27/7/1901	Bradford Daily Telegraph. Bradford Liberals picnic.
25/4/1902	Shipley Times and Express. Letter about Improvement of Shipley Glen.
21/5/1902	Bradford Daily Telegraph. Large crowds.
30/6/1902	Yorkshire Evening Post. Shipley Glen a strong attraction.

22/8/1902	Bradford Daily Telegraph. Donkeys at Vulcan House.
23/10/1902	Yorkshire Post and Leeds Intelligencer. Condition of approach roads concern.
11/4/1903	Bradford Daily Telegraph. Trains and tramcars full and attractions on the Glen receiving much patronage.
30/6/1903	Leeds Mercury. Ruskin Hall Movement Gathering on Shipley Glen.
24/4/1904	Bradford Daily Telegraph. Large number of refreshment stalls and entertainments. Switchback very busy.
15/9/1904	Leeds Mercury. Bradford Corporation visit to inspect site of proposed new roads.
17/10/1904	Bradford Daily Telegraph. 100 unemployed required for building of new road.
19/10/1904	Bradford Daily Telegraph. 50 unemployed commenced work on building new road.
17/3/1905	Shipley Times and Express. Mr Roberts Cinematographic Exhibition by Vulcan Bioscope Co. He is the son of Elizabeth Perry by her first husband.
16/5/1905	Shipley Times and Express. Mrs Perry's Vulcan House Adverts.
9/6/1905	Shipley Times and Express Lucy Hall Farm Teas Advert.
23/6/1905	Shipley Times and Express. Hartley's Japanese Gardens Advert.
26/8/1905	The Era. Wanted 10,000 feet of second-hand film, B Roberts, Vulcan Bioscope Co, Vulcan House.
15/12/1905	Shipley Times and Express. Vulcan Cinematographic Exhibition.
13/4/1906	Shipley Times and Express. Elizabeth Perry summoned and fined for trading on a Sunday.

20/4/1906	Wharfedale and Airedale Observer. Big holiday crowds at Easter.
25/5/1906	Shipley Times and Express. Shipley Glen Open Air Concerts near Switchback - Bracken Hall Orchestral Band.
1/6/1906	Shipley Times and Express. Advert for Glen Concerts in a marquee near Switchback organized by Mr W. M. Marsden.
8/6/1906	Shipley Times and Express In a field near the switchback at Shipley Glen Mr W. M. Marsden has created a spacious marquee for the purpose of holding promenade concerts during the season. A pretty little stage has been erected.
13/7/1906	Shipley Times and Express. Bracken Hall Grounds Grand Sunday Concerts.
5/4/1907	Bradford Daily Telegraph. Attack on W. M. Marsden by showman demanding water.
5/4/1907	Wharfedale and Airedale Advertiser. Large numbers at Glen and fairground.
31/5/1907	Shipley Times and Express. Primitive Methodist Church Centenary Camp.
16/1/1908	Yorkshire Evening Post. Easter Carnival. Grounds to be let for steam roundabouts at the White House.
4/4/1908	Votes for Women. Large suffragette rally.
10/4/1908	Shipley Times and Express. Large suffragette rally.
4/9/1908	Socialist demonstration held on the plateau.
12/4/1909	Leeds Mercury. Large Easter crowd.
21/5/1909	Shipley Times and Express. Free Trade Demonstration
12/7/1909	Leeds Mercury. Yorkshire Esperanto Federation picnic at Crook Farm.
9/8/1909	Budget League rally at Glen.

19/2/1909	Shipley Times and Express. Tom Hartley - Plans for one storey bungalow in grounds of Japanese Gardens considered.
26/3/1910	Yorkshire Post and Leeds Intelligencer. Easter - Large numbers at Shipley Glen.
17/5/1910	Yorkshire Post and Leeds Intelligencer. Advert - Tramway to be sold off as owner wishing to retire.
18/6/1910	Burnley Gazette. Employees picnic at Shipley Glen.
12/8/1910	Yorkshire Post and Leeds Intelligencer. Many people visited the Glen and Ilkley Moor.
15/4/1911	Leeds Mercury. Constant stream of visitors to Shipley Glen then over the moors to Ilkley. Roundabouts etc at Easter Fair reaped a rich harvest.
11/8/1911	Wharfedale and Airedale Observer. No roundabouts or joy wheels on Bank Holiday Monday. Many people seen crossing the moor to Ilkley.
22/11/1911	Yorkshire Evening Post. Shipley Glen Garden City Scheme - Prod Lane and Lucy Hall Estate.
16 /1/1912	National Probate Calendar. Elizabeth Perry of Vulcan House dies.
9/4/1912	Yorkshire Post. Tram cars were besieged early en route for Shipley Glen or the moors beyond.
24/7/1912	Yorkshire Evening Post. Suffragette rally.
23/9/1912	Yorkshire Evening Post article identifying Switchback Railway, Cable Cars, Camera Obscura, Swings and the Picture Palace. I pointed out the Switchback railway, the cable cars, the camera obscura, the picture palace and all the other attractions.
25/3/1913	Leeds Mercury. Largest crowd for an Easter Monday Fair estimated at 100,000 - roundabouts reaped a rich harvest.
2/5/1913	Shipley Times and Express. Shipley Glen - Roads cut up by heavy traction engines.

9/5/1913	Shipley Times and Express. Comment by Bradford Corporation on damage caused by heavy traffic during Easter Fair. Statement - No ground to be let at Brackenhall Green or on the Common for apparatus mechanically worked. No roundabouts at the Easter Fair from 1914.
13/5/1913	Leeds Mercury. Tramway from Bradford broke all records - Shipley Glen and the moors were the destination of most travellers.
30/5/2013	Shipley Times and Express. Advertisement - Sale of house and shop Vulcan House. Benjamin A. W. Roberts advertised the Pleasure Grounds and Refreshment rooms, sweet shop, photographers shop, large tent used for cinematographic shows, swings, roundabout, and the "contrivance known as the Cape to Cairo railway" (Aerial Glide).
6/6/2013	Shipley Times and Express. First Advertisement for Shipley Glen Wonderland by J. T. Clark - part of Japanese Gardens sold by Tom Hartley.
18/6/1913	Shipley Times and Express. Advertisement for Coopers Tea Gardens/Rooms and Glen Toffee.
30/6/1913	Leeds Mercury. Madam De Laurie, Palmist and Clairvoyant - Horoscope Interviews at the Japanese Gardens.
3/4/1914	Shipley Times and Express. (The Shipley Glen Carnival) Roundabouts banned.
3/4/1914	Shipley Times and Express - Local Notes and Table Talk - The switchback railway originally constructed for the Saltaire Exhibition in 1887, which was afterwards bought by a Baildon "syndicate" for £100 and re-erected at a cost of about another £100 on land adjoining the plateau at Shipley Glen, came under the auctioneers hammer last Friday night. Several bids were made for the lot which was eventually knocked

down for £68 to Mr Timothy Wilson, landlord of the Roebuck Inn. Twenty seven years ago the switchback cost the exhibition authorities about £500. Later withdrawn but sold in 1917 (see below).

17/4/1914	Leeds Mercury. A crowd roughly estimated at 70,000 had "invaded" the Glen on Easter Monday.
17/4/1914	Shipley Times and Express - (Shipley Glen at Easter - The Reconstructed Fair) - White House. Shipley Glen crowded nonwithstanding the exclusion of the roundabouts. Second fair at the White House did not prove a success.
1914	Tom Hartley retires from Japanese Gardens.
27/5/1914	J. T. Clark Shipley Glen Wonderland advertisement... cafe, swings, grotto and boating (Japanese Gardens).
21/5/1915	Shipley Times and Express. Shipley Volunteers Corps manoeuvres on Baildon Green and Shipley Glen.
25/5/1915	Leeds Mercury. Glorious weather drew thousands to the Glen and moors.
11/6/1915	Shipley Times and Express. Picnic for families of fighting men picnic at Shipley Glen.
14/6/1915	Leeds Mercury. Volunteers Corps manoeuvres at Golcar Farm.
22/4/1916	Leeds Mercury. Good Friday exodus to Shipley Glen and the moors.
4/8/1916	Shipley Times and Express. Anti Conscription Peace meeting at Shipley Glen.
29/6/1917	Shipley Times and Express. Switchback - Auction notice for three cars, iron rails, wood and register turnstile.
13/7/1917	Shipley Times and Express. Switchback sold by Bradford Auctioneers C. W. Bell to John Smith, Scrap Metal Dealer for £99.

3/8/1917	Shipley Times and Express. Tramway offered for sale after 23 years - Property withdrawn.
3/8/1917	Shipley Times and Express. Switchback removed.
5/4/1918	Shipley Times and Express. Changes at Shipley Glen, gone are the toboggan, aerial flight, switchback and roundabouts etc.
4/3/1919	Yorkshire Post and Leeds Intelligencer. Shipley Glen Tramway for immediate sale due to deteriorating health of owner...valuable undertaking in full working order.
25/4/1919	Shipley Times and Express. Glen busy.
13/6/1919	Shipley Times and Express. Shipley Glen amongst principal Bank Holiday attractions and well in the running with best of the West Yorkshire resorts.
15/8/1919	Shipley Times and Express. A first impression of Shipley Glen - tearooms, pleasure gardens and Japanese Garden and walks to Ilkley.
1919	Sam Wilson retired from Tramway.
7/4/1920	Yorkshire Evening Post. This Easter there have been queues for the hill tramway, the tearooms and of children at the donkey rides.
28/5/1920	Shipley Times and Express. Amusements and tuck shops well patronized and family picnic parties enjoyed.
1/4/1921	Shipley Times and Express. Article. Up to WWI Shipley Glen boasted a fair of the old fashioned kind... Now however things have altered, the fair has deteriorated and its glory died...

BIBLIOGRAPHY

Cattell. A.H. (2011 pp94-115) *Bingley and Surrounds - Forgotten Moments from History.*

Conlin. C. (2012 pp207) *The Pleasure Garden - From Vauxhall to Coney Island.*

Cudworth. W. (1875 pp336) *Round About Bradford.*

Dingle. A. E. (1980) *The Campaign of Prohibition in Victorian Britain.*

Easdown. M. (2012 pp22) *Amusement Park Rides.*

Frost. T. (1875 Chapter 11) *The Old Showmen.*

Harrison. W. (1997) *Day's Awake - Childhood Memories of Bingley.*

Kane. J. (2016 pp13) *The Architecture of Pleasure - British Amusement Parks 1930-1939.*

Leak. M. J. (2003) *100 Years at Shipley Glen - The Story of the Glen Tramway.*

Leak. M.J. (2003) and updated for Shipley Glen Preservation Co Ltd (2016) *The Shipley Glen Tramway - Its Social History since 1895 and its mechanics.*

Navickas. K (2016) *The Protest and Politics of Space and Place 1789-1849.*

Paley. W. (1912 pp7) *Baildon and the Baildons; a History of a Yorkshire Manor and Family.*

Roberts. M. (2008 pp93) *Political Movements in Urban England.*

Simon. J. (2013 pp109) *The Rough Guide to Yorkshire.*

Taylor. D. (1986 pp188-190) Yorkshire Archaeological Journal Volume 58 *Yorkshire Amusement Parks and Gardens.*

Varo. S. (1985) *Shipley Glen Ramble.*

Newspaper Sources Quoted in the Main Text
Bradford Daily Telegraph
Bradford Observer
Bradford Times
Craven Herald
Ilkley Gazette and Wharfedale Advertiser
Leeds Mercury
Leeds Times
Pall Mall Gazette
Shipley Times and Express
Target
Telegraph and Argus
The Illustrated Mail
Wharfedale and Airedale Observer
Yorkshire Evening Post
Yorkshire Post and Leeds Intelligencer

Other Useful Sources of Information

Burrows. D (1985) *Baildon - a look at the past*

Burrows. D (1985) *Saltaire - a look at the past*

Historic England (2015) Historic Amusement Parks and Fairground Rides www.academia.edu/29729064/Historic_Amusement_Parks.

The National Fairground and Circus Archive at the University of Sheffield (2018) www.sheffield.ac.uk/nfca

Radice. G. (2003) A Tale of Shipley Glen - The Mike Short Interview www.joylandbooks.com/.../articles/taleofshipleyglen.htm

Slessor. W. (2011) DVD Shipley Glen and Baildon Moor - The Story www.slessors.co.uk

Yorkshire Film Archive www.yorkshirefilmarchive.com/film/easter-shipley-glen-1912

Bingley History Series

For information on Alan's previous books, visit the
Bingley History Series website

Sir Titus Salt and Sons
A Farming Legacy

This book builds on recent research by local
historians and two members of the Salt family
to show that besides Manufacturing, Sir Titus
Salt and four of his sons were also involved in
Agriculture and Farming.

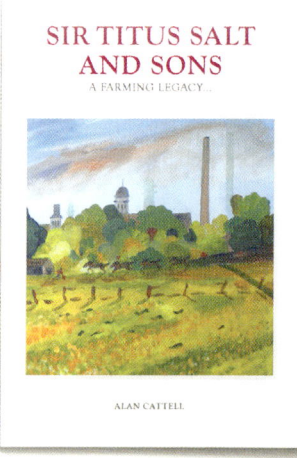

Bingley -
A Living History

Discover the changing historical face of
Bingley between 1800 - 2016
A fascinating compilation of research, interesting
narrative and range of photographs which give a
real sense of time and place.

*❝ I never knew any of the history of the Bingley Allotments opposite Beckfoot
School until I got a book - Bingley and Surrounds - Forgotten Moments
from History by Alan Cattell out of Bingley library recently. I found it
fascinating. There is much more to Bingley than first meets the eye! ❞
N. Smith*

For further information, visit Alan's website below
www.bingleyhistoryseries.co.uk